ISBN 978-1-330-19011-1
PIBN 10048546

1 MONTH OF
FREE
READING

at

www.ForgottenBooks.com

By purchasing this book you are eligible for one month membership to ForgottenBooks.com, giving you unlimited access to our entire collection of over 700,000 titles via our web site and mobile apps.

To claim your free month visit:

www.forgottenbooks.com/free48546

A SHORT POPULAR HISTORY OF CRETE

A

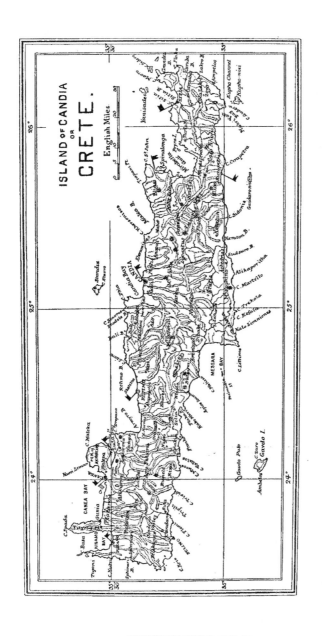

A SHORT POPULAR
HISTORY OF CRETE

BY

J. H. FREESE, M.A.

LATE FELLOW OF ST. JOHN'S COLLEGE, CAMBRIDGE

WITH INTRODUCTION

By P. W. CLAYDEN

SANS PEUR ET
SANS REPROCHE

L & N

THIRD EDITION

LONDON

JARROLD & SONS, 10 & 11, WARWICK LANE, E.C.

1897

PREFATORY NOTE.

THE compiler of this little book desires to acknowledge his special obligations to the following works amongst a large number of others which have been consulted : —

Louis Lacroix, *Iles de la Grèce* (*Univers pittoresque.* vol. xxxviii.).

G. Finlay, *History of Greece.*

P. Daru, *Histoire de Venise.*

Von Hammer, *History of the Ottoman Empire.*

Larousse, *Dictionnaire Universel.*

Encyclopædia Britannica, *Article " Crete."*

F. Bamberg, *Geschichte der Orientalischen Angelegenheit im Zeitraume der Pariser und des Berliner Friedens*

E. Hertslet, *The Map of Europe by Treaty.*

R. Pashley, *Travels in Crete.*

The Gazetteer of the World.

A. F. Yule, *A Little Light on Cretan Insurrections.*

W. J. Stillman, *The Cretan Insurrection of* 1866–1868.

Fauriel, *Chants populaires de la Grèce moderne.*

Elpis Melena, *Kreta-Biene.*

A Passow, *Carmina Popularia Græciæ Recentioris*

CONTENTS

CHAPTER   PAGE

INTRODUCTION 7

I. THE ISLAND OF CRETE: GEOGRAPHICAL AND PHYSICAL
FEATURES 25

II. ANCIENT CRETE, TO THE TIME OF ITS CONQUEST BY THE
ROMANS 32

III. THE HISTORY OF CRETE, FROM THE TIME OF ITS CON-
QUEST BY THE ROMANS TO ITS CAPTURE BY THE
TURKS 48

IV. THE HISTORY OF THE ISLAND, FROM ITS CAPTURE BY
THE TURKS TO THE PRESENT TIME ... 73

V. GREEK HETÆRIÆ AND THE WAR OF INDEPENDENCE 112

VI. CRETAN SONGS AND LEGENDS 133

INTRODUCTION.

FOR many weeks I have been receiving from all parts of the kingdom requests for information on the subject of Crete and the relations of the Cretans with the kingdom of Greece. It has been impossible to meet this demand, because the Cretan question and the action of the Greek Government and people can only be explained by telling the island story, and no brief but sufficient summary of Cretan history was to be found. This want is supplied by Mr. Freese in the following chapters, which give an account of the geographical and physical features of the island, sketch its political and social life from the earliest times till now, and show what have been the struggles and aspirations of the whole Hellenic people. It is impossible, without such a glance back over their stormy and suffering past, to understand the position, or to enter into the feelings and aspirations of the Greek nation or their Cretan brothers. Crete has been a martyr island. It had a thousand years of changeful history before the Christian era, and, making allowance for a few centuries of peace and prosperity, it may fairly be said to have had a thousand years of struggle and suffering in Christian times. It lies, as it were, on the border line between East and West, between Christian civilization and the semi-barbarism of Islam, and the tides of Mohammedan conquest and Christian victory have swept backwards and forwards over it for centuries. Its people are therefore what ages of conflict have made them. Wherever the Ottoman Turk rules, barbarism gains on civilization, commerce decays, agriculture is neglected, and all the humanities, to use the Scottish phrase, die of inanition. It is not the fault of the Cretan peasant, therefore, if, like Othello, he is rude in speech—

"And little bless'd with the set phrase of peace ; "

for he must say, with the Moor—

"And little of this great world can I speak,
More than pertains to feats of broil and battle."

Ten times within the present century the Cretans have been driven to revolt by the intolerable oppression of their alien rulers, and from the time when Europe forced them back under Turkish rule in 1830 to the present moment they have known little else than "broil and battle." The sixty-six years since Leopold refused the Crown of Greece, because this essential part of the Greek kingdom had been forcibly rent from it and re-enslaved, have seen seven rebellions, two of which lasted for a couple of years or more. That of last spring lingered on till the late summer, and after a brief time of comparative quiet blazed up again early in this year, and has brought the active interference of the Greeks and the present war.

The condition of Crete for eighteen months before the outbreak of these latest troubles is fully described in the detailed despatches of Consul Biliotti. During that period the consul sent home more than two hundred and forty letters and telegrams, in which may be read the story of Cretan life from day to day. It is all along a story of disorder and discontent, of pillage and murder. Month after month his letters convey the most serious warnings of coming trouble. A mere glance at the Blue Book (Turkey, No. 7, 1896) shows the disturbed condition of the country. "Murder of Christians by Mussulmans" is the burden of its index pages. Lists of murders and outrages are sent home by the consul from time to time, and on the 3rd of October, 1895, he reports to Lord Salisbury that he has been told that the low class of Mussulmans are speaking of making the Christians in Crete "repent of any concessions which the Sultan may grant in Asia." On the 21st of November he writes, that the situation, "in the opinion, not only of the native Christians, but in that of the Mussulmans themselves, is now quite intolerable;" and on the 3rd of December Lord Salisbury, writing to Sir Philip Currie, urges him to impress on the Porte "the danger of serious trouble unless some remedial measures are soon adopted." But Sir Philip Currie is instructed to do his spiriting gently, to be careful to assure the Porte that "Her Majesty's Government are actuated by no wish to interfere in the affairs of Crete, or to suggest any course of action, but that they desire only in a spirit of friendship that the Sultan's Government should anticipate, and thus avert, complications to which a continuance of the present disorders will assuredly give rise." This "spirit of friendship" was to be shown towards the government of a man whose hands were already red with the blood of thousands of Christians in Armenia, and who was at that moment preparing one of the most bloody and cruel massacres in the whole history of the Christian Church. The appeal had no effect. Sir Philip Currie wrote on the 18th of December, that the Turkish Government was "incapable of taking any effectual steps to remedy the present state of things in Crete, or to avert the insurrection which, it is generally believed, will break out in the spring."

All the winter Consul Biliotti kept Lord Salisbury informed of every detail of public affairs, as fully as though Crete was an integral part of the British Empire. In February, 1896, the racial murders began to be frequent, and the catalogue sent home in March and April shows a state of complete disorder. On the 7th of March, Consul Biliotti gave an account of various disturbances and sufferings, and added, " All these details are certainly known at Constantinople, but nothing is done to find a remedy for a state of things which, before long, must fatally lead to a general outbreak, and disorders which may exceed even those of the year 1889." So matters drifted on till May. All this time Carathéodori Pasha, a Greek Christian, was the Governor ; but the Porte refused him the means of paying his police, and the commander of the Turkish troops mocked his authority and frustrated his efforts. In March, 1896, he was recalled, and Consul Biliotti reported that even the Mussulmans deeply deplored his departure. His recall was the sign that the farce of keeping to the reforms which the Powers had exacted, was at an end. Turkhan Pasha, a Mussulman, was sent to reign in his stead, and Consul Biliotti telegraphed on the 24th of March that attempts at murder and murders were daily committed by Mussulmans against Christians, and that on that day the Christians in Canea had not opened their shops, as three attempts at murder had taken place on the day before. The whole island now fell into a state of anarchy; and early in May Turkhan Pasha adjourned the General Assembly till August. On the 21st of that month the Foreign Minister of the Porte told Mr. Herbert at Constantinople that the position of affairs in Crete was very bad. Turkhan Pasha was recalled, and a soldier, Abdullah Pasha, was put in his place. The next day Turkhan Pasha got orders from Constantinople to convoke the General Assembly for the 28th, but the Grand Vizier told Mr. Herbert that the demands of the Cretans could not be granted, that the convocation of the Assembly would have but little effect, and that he feared order could only be restored by military measures. On the very day of the despatch of this telegram from Constantinople, the military measures were effectually prepared for by a rising of the Mussulman population, and a massacre of Christians in Canea.

The demands of the Cretans, which the Turks determined to resist, were substantially that the Pact or Convention of Halepa, which is fully described by Mr. Freese in his fourth chapter, should be carried out. They asked that the gendarmerie should be composed of Cretans, and not of Albanians and others from different parts of the Empire; that the Custom-house administration and revenue should be handed over to the Cretans; that Turkish correspondence clerks should be done away with; and that the old system of jurisprudence should be restored. The Porte, however, as Mr. Block inferred from a conversation he had with the Grand Vizier, had resolved on military measures, and Mr. Herbert knew so well what this determination meant that he telegraphed from Constantinople to Lord Salisbury :

"The Turkish Government, according to all the information I receive, are determined to quell the insurrection in Crete by force, with their customary severity. I think, therefore, in view of this probability and the Zeitoun experience, that we should be very careful how we allow our consul to give any guarantees as to conditions being carried out by the Sublime Porte."

This warning of the untrustworthy character of the Turkish Government was acted on. Consul Biliotti was instructed not to accept responsibility for any conditions, but to confine himself to bringing about negotiations and settling the preliminaries of an arrangement. This order to our consul was repeated, and similar orders were sent by all the Powers to their representatives. The consuls telegraphed for warships, and warships were sent. Meanwhile reports were sent home that the Porte was shipping troops for Crete, and Mr. Herbert's fears of a repetition in the Greek island of the Zeitoun severities were shared by all the Powers as well as by the people and the Government of Greece. Greece was deeply stirred. It seemed to the Greek people to be their duty to step in and shield the Cretans from the vengeance of the Assassin of the Armenians. Count Goluchowski, the Austrian Minister, expressed to our Ambassador at Vienna, Sir E. Monson, the fear that events had gone to such lengths that an irresistible popular current might carry away the King of Greece and his Government, and he significantly added, " The blame for the present situation lies entirely with the Turks themselves, and it will be impossible for Greece to stand aloof if acts of savagery take place in the island." Greece, however, possessed her soul in patience. She took the advice of the Powers, and in so doing let a great opportunity slip. Crete was ready to fall into her hands, and Count Goluchowski said that she would have had much European sympathy if she interfered to stop the savagery. There was everything to justify her interference. Consul Biliotti telegraphed to Lord Salisbury in June : " Pillage and fire mark the passage of the troops." The Christians in the interior, however, held their own, and the efforts of the Turks to conquer them entirely failed. They had themselves struck the blow and won their freedom. If at this moment Greece had been allowed to step in, the union of Crete to the Hellenic Kingdom might have been accomplished amid general consent.

The Greeks, however, have a watchful enemy in Russia. They stand in Russia's way. A strong Hellenic kingdom would not only bar her progress to the warmer seas, but might compete with her for the old capital of the Byzantine Empire. The political superstition of " the integrity and independence of the Ottoman Empire " has now its headquarters at St. Petersburg, while Austria professes allegiance to it, and France bows the knee to any idol Russia may set up. M. Hanotaux told Mr. Howard on the 8th of July, that if the Powers could smother the Cretan question they would do a good work. So Prince Lobanoff thought, and he induced Austria to propose the blockade of Crete, to prevent the importation of arms or volunteers from Greece. Lord Salisbury made a fitting reply to this proposal. In a despatch to Mr. Gosselin, on the 29th of July, he said that he had told the German Ambassador—

That I saw no prospect of Her Majesty's Government being able to adhere to this suggestion. They had always declined to intervene in cases of civil strife between a Government and its subjects, and their objection would be accentuated by the fact that they would be intervening in opposition to Christian insurgents who had very solid grievances to complain of. After what had taken place in Armenia during the winter, it was difficult to count on the moderation or clemency with which the Turkish Government would be likely to use any victory it might achieve, and Her Majesty's Government, therefore, shrank from taking part by material intervention in the work of restoring the authority of the Sultan, when they had at their disposal no means of insuring that the restored authority would be exerted with moderation and justice.

The German Ambassador thereupon reminded Lord Salisbury of the Greek blockade, instituted when Mr. Gladstone was Prime Minister, and asked him whether that was not a precedent for the blockade of Crete. But Lord Salisbury says—

I replied that the distinction between the two appeared to me to be very marked. If Greece were to assume a hostile attitude to the Turkish Government, and make any aggression upon the independence or integrity of the Turkish Empire, the collective guarantee into which the Powers entered at the Treaty of Paris would become a matter of serious consideration. . . . But the question submitted by Count Goluchowski was not that of coercing the Government of Greece; it was that of taking part against the Cretan insurgents. I added, as a secondary objection to the proposal, that I very much doubted its success. It was no easy matter to guard a littoral so indented as that of Crete, and to prevent the blockade being broken by small fishing-boats from the neighbouring coasts of Africa or of Greece; and the blockade would not be an easy one to maintain in the face of the weather which usually prevailed in the seas between Crete and Greece in the early part of the autumn. Some of the Powers were now urging a blockade on the ground that it did not consist with their dignity to allow their recommendations to be set at naught ; but I feared that if the blockade was tried and failed they would think it still less consistent with their dignity to acquiesce in such a result, and the question of military occupation, with all the rivalries and entanglements which it would involve, would then be forced on us for decision. (Turkey, No. 7, 1896, p. 231.)

This admirable despatch settled the whole question. Nothing more was heard of the proposed blockade, though Count Goluchowski was " extremely agitated and impressed by the difficulties of the situation " when Lord Salisbury's wise decision was communicated to him. He thought it might lead to war ; and hinted that it "would certainly intensify the suspicions already entertained of British policy." Lord Salisbury, however, refused to move, and said that " it was not an even-handed proceeding to give the Sultan the assistance of the ships which would intervene by force, while giving the Cretans the assistance of a Commission which could only intervene by representations." He repeated this reply in answer to an alternative proposal that the Sultan should close the ports, and the ships of the Powers should watch the ports for him. The balance, he said, was not even. " It was deeds on one side, and mere words on the other. The exercise of force would not be sufficiently balanced by the presentation of remonstrances." He added that " it was impossible that Great Britain should take part in proceedings intended to paralyze the action of the insurgents, unless by the exercise of force on the other side also adequate guarantees were taken for the future good government of the island."

As the British Minister was thus firm, the other Powers and the Sultan were obliged to give way. The Porte adopted its usual tactics of delay. Prince Lobanoff talked about "a political volcano bursting out" if the Powers failed to act together, and Count Goluchowski, down to the middle of August, pressed his scheme for the blockade, but Lord Salisbury was firm. In the end a settlement was come to, which received the signatures of the six Powers on the 25th of August, and of the Sultan's representative on the 27th; and on the 5th of September Consul Biliotti wrote that "both Christians and Mussulmans are very happy to be led out of the untenable position in which they were placed." He thought that more good-will was to be expected on the part of the Mussulmans than of the Christians themselves in carrying out the new organization. The consuls of the Great Powers communicated the scheme to the Christian deputies, and in informing the Governor of what they had done, made complaint of the massacre close to the gates of Canea, and close to a military post, of many unarmed and peaceable Christians, "who had only returned to their village on the invitation of the authorities, and on the assurance that they would enjoy the most complete security." The Consuls told the Governor that these disorders made them fear that the Government was powerless to maintain public order, and threatened to appeal to the Sultan if this disorder was not stopped at once. A fortnight later Berovitch Pasha, a Christian, was appointed Governor, and hope revived. The scheme he had to administer was one of autonomy. There was to be a Commission to reform the Tribunals, and another to reorganize the gendarmerie under European officers. The elections were to be ordered and the Assembly convoked within six months.

For a brief month or two there was much exultation among Lord Salisbury's political friends over this diplomatic success. It was held by them to condone his failure in Armenia, and to show what the Concert of Europe could do when Great Britain was faithful to it. On paper Crete was free, and yet the integrity of the Turkish Empire had been kept. In Crete itself there was a brief period of calm. The Christian deputies issued an appeal to Christians and Mussulmans, "children of the same country, belonging to the same race," to let the work of peace be henceforth their only strife. The Christians, who had fled to Greece in thousands, began to return; and the Mussulmans, who had taken possession of the abandoned homes of the fugitives, were urged to restore the property to its rightful owners. There was some friction over this restoration, but early in October, Consul Sir Alfred Biliotti wrote that there was a strong wish on the part of Mussulmans and Christians to live in peace. A most productive olive crop was gathered in, and the towns began to assume their usual aspect. There was, however, an uneasy feeling that the proposed reforms would never be carried out. The Christian Governor soon found that he was nobody, and that the commander of the Turkish troops was supreme. It was nearly Christmas before the organization of the gendarmerie was begun, or the

B

Commission on the Tribunals was at work. A whisper went through the Mussulman community that the reforms were to be resisted, and they openly boasted that the interference of the Powers in Crete would be as futile as it had been in Armenia. It was not till the middle of January, 1897, that the Porte finally accepted the scheme of the European Commission on the gendarmerie, and the Mussulmans were advised from Constantinople not to allow it to be carried out. At the end of January a well-known Christian was murdered outside the gates of Canea, and the Mussulman mob made a night attack on the populous Christian village of Galata, an hour away, which the Christians repulsed, though two hundred of their houses were burned. The Christians in other villages flew to arms, and in the country outnumbered their enemies. In the coast towns, however, the Mussulmans were in the ascendant, and the consuls at Canea sent for the warships, and offered the Christians of that place an asylum on board. On the 4th of February, the Mussulman mob of Canea, aided by the Turkish soldiers, attacked the Christian quarter, committing frightful atrocities—in one case baking nine Christians in an oven—and ending by setting fire to the city. After some hesitation, during which the Christian quarter was destroyed, the ships sent fire-engines and stayed the flames, the mob plundering the houses which the fire spared. At night there was not a Christian in the town, but the ships were crowded with Christian refugees. All over the island the Mussulman population were in arms against the Christians; and the Turkish military authorities, who had pushed the Governor aside, supplied their co-religionists with arms, or gave them active co-operation. It was the Constantinople massacre on a smaller scale.

On the day after the burning of Canea a meeting of Cretan deputies and chiefs at Halepa proclaimed the union of the island with Greece. The Christians everywhere fought under the Greek flag, and the Christian Governor of the island took refuge at the Hellenic consulate at Halepa. These events roused indignation all over Europe, and excited the Greek people to frenzy. The Porte made arrangements to send troops to Crete, and the Greek Government resolved to stop them. The time had come which Count Goluchowski had anticipated, when the Greeks could no longer be prevented from intervening. The Concert of Europe had failed. Another specious scheme of autonomy had broken down, and the Cretans had called on the mother country to aid them in effecting complete emancipation from their treacherous tyrant. The Christian insurgents had found the Powers unwilling or unable to give them the slightest security, and they had taken their defence into their own hands. In this supreme crisis they called on the Greeks to help them. Greece flew to their aid, and its Government explained and justified its action in a few dignified words—

Events in Crete have brought that unfortunate island to a state of anarchy, and the lives and possessions of the Christians are exposed to the fury of a fanatic populace. The Greek Government could no longer tolerate this lamentable situation of the Christian population to whom we are united by the sacred ties of religion. They have consequently decided to send an army corps to occupy the island and re-establish order and peace.

Colonel Vassos, aide-de-camp to the King, was despatched with four battalions of Greek troops, and his instructions were—

You will land with the troops under your orders at the most favourable point ; you will occupy the island in the name of King George, and you will raise his flag on the fortress of which you will take possession. All your actions shall be accomplished in conformity with Greek laws in the name of King George, and on the responsibility of his Government. As soon as you have landed you will publish a proclamation announcing to the Cretan people the occupation of the island by the Greek troops.

This heroic step was resented by the Powers. They could not keep order, nor prevent the most revolting atrocities, but they preferred anarchy and massacre to a peace and quiet secured by Greeks. Prince George and his ships were warned off, but despised the warning, and though Colonel Vassos was allowed to land, he was regarded as an enemy. He met with an enthusiastic welcome from the whole Christian population, who rallied at once to his standard and hailed him as a national deliverer. Everywhere in the interior the Greeks and Christians were successful, and drove the Turks towards the sea. By the 20th of February the Turks were sorely pressed, and the five admirals sent an ultimatum to the victorious patriots, threatening to fire on them if they approached Canea. On Sunday, the 21st, the patriots joined issue with the Turks on the hills east of the town. "The Turkish reply," said the *Daily News* correspondent, who was present, "was feeble, and it was obvious that the Turks must abandon their position if pressed." The fleets, however, interfered to save them. The ships fired seventy shells, forty of

which were from British guns. Three Cretans were
killed and fifteen wounded, among whom were three
nuns. "The Turks, encouraged by the fleets, now
opened a lively fusilade, while the Cretans were carrying off their dead. The Cretans made no reply. The
whole performance," adds the correspondent, "was a
somewhat melancholy and degrading spectacle." On
the next day a Turkish ship in Suda Bay and the
Turkish soldiers at the arsenal fired at the same body
of patriots though the white flag was hoisted, but the
Cretans did not reply. On Wednesday night an in-
cendiary fire, kindled by Mussulmans with the hope of
plunder, broke out at the Government Palace in Canea,
and destroyed that last vestige of Turkish rule.

The agitation which these events produced all over
Europe woke up the slumbering Powers. Their impulse was to blame Greece. Mr. Gladstone described
the bombardment as filling up the measure of their
dishonour; and Lord Salisbury announced that the
Powers had resolved on keeping Crete for the Sultan
by another measure of "autonomy." The Greeks were
to be compelled to withdraw; but the Turkish troops
were to stay for a while "for reasons of police." This
proposal to keep the cut-throats to look after the safety
of their victims, met with general disapproval. The
admirals occupied Canea and Candia to keep peace;
but in the interior the Christians carried all before them.
On the 2nd of March the Powers sent an ultimatum to
Greece. They declared that they could not allow
Greece to annex Crete at present, but would themselves
give it a complete scheme of autonomy. They
"invited" Greece to withdraw her troops from the

island, and her fleet from its waters, and added, "In case of refusal" the Powers are irrevocably determined to hesitate at no measure of compulsion if, on the expiry of a period of six days, the withdrawal of the ships and troops be not effected." A courteous note informed the Porte of the proposed autonomy, and suggested the concentration of the Turkish troops within the fortified towns. At the end of the six days, the Greek Government sent an argumentative reply, but did not withdraw the ships or the troops, and the six Powers began at once to hesitate as to the measure of compulsion to apply. They allowed the consuls to announce the proposed autonomy to the people of Crete, and the people at once rejected it. The French Chamber was told that Crete was to be rigidly blockaded first, and afterwards certain points on the Greek coast, and that in Crete itself an additional force of five or six hundred men was to be landed by each of the Powers. The blockade of Crete was begun on the 21st of March, but that of Greece was postponed, and Colonel Vassos held the whole interior of the island, and at the end of March was actually governing it in the name of King George. Fighting, however, went on wherever the Turks and Christian insurgents met, the admirals always taking the side of the Turks, and again bombarding the Christians at Malaxa, near Suda, on the 27th of March. At Canea the Cretans saw other signs of fraternization between their ostensible deliverers and their old oppressors. When the Seaforth Highlanders landed at Canea, the Turkish soldiers and their officers gave them an effusive welcome, and conducted them to the Turkish barracks with musical honours. A few days later an international force of British, French, Italians, and Russians, marched out of Canea with the Turkish troops to occupy a fort above the town. In spite of all this pro-Turkish action, Colonel Vassos keeps the interior for King George, while the international fleets and soldiers hold the coast for Turkey. The promised autonomy has slipped out of sight.

Meanwhile the stress of the conflict between freedom and the vilest despotism on earth has shifted to another field. Both sides have felt that the interference of the European Powers in Crete would force them to fight out the issue on other soil. There were rumours all through March of the concentration of Turkish troops in Thessaly and Epirus, and of the gathering of irregular forces in the interests of Greece. On the 9th of April several bands of irregulars crossed the Macedonian frontier after a solemn religious service among the olive trees. The Greek Government naturally repudiated any responsibility for their action, and the Powers looked on incapable or irresolute. Neither the Greeks nor the Turks wanted war, and there is every reason to believe that the Sultan and King George were equally anxious to come to an agreement and be at peace. The Powers, however, at the dictation of Russia, forbade the negotiations ; and on Easter Sunday, Europe was startled by the news that, on the day before, Turkey had declared war against Greece, and that a great battle had been fought on the same night. How this sudden resolution of the Turks was brought about is at present one of the secrets of diplomacy. It fell on the European Concert like a thunderbolt. For months the people of England, France, and Italy had been assured that their

Governments kept in the Concert with the three despotic Powers in the interests of Peace. It was to give Crete her freedom, and to preserve the peace of Europe, that the guns of Christian nations were fired on Christian patriots fighting against oppression. But the crime against religion and humanity has been committed in vain. Crete is not free, and war is raging on European soil. In this war, the Concert of Europe acts for the Turk by holding Crete in his interest, and the long struggle of the Christian races, not only for " freedom to worship God," but for security against the worst crimes of barbarian passion, might, in Crete at least, come to a triumphant end, were not the British fleet in Russia's keeping, and the British people powerless in Lord Salisbury's subservient hands.

P. W. CLAYDEN.

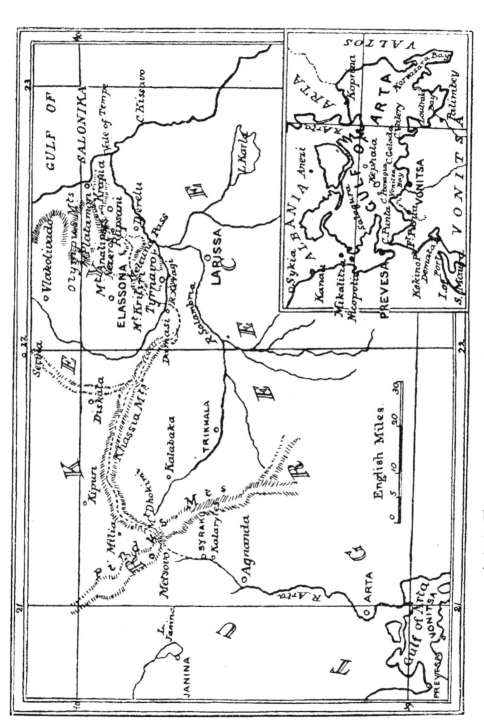

MAP of the SEAT of WAR.

A SHORT POPULAR
HISTORY OF CRETE.

CHAPTER I.

THE ISLAND OF CRETE : GEOGRAPHICAL AND PHYSICAL FEATURES.

CRETE, the ancient Crētē, called by the Turks Gireed, and commonly by Europeans Candia, a name which is not recognized upon the island itself, is one of the largest islands of the Mediterranean. In ancient times it was also called Macaronēsos (fortunate island) and Aëria (airy), owing to its fertility and beautiful climate, and Dolichē (long), from its shape. The etymology of the ancient name itself cannot be satisfactorily settled. According to the ecclesiastical historian, Eusebius, it was so called from its first king, Cres, a son of Zeus ; * while another Greek historian, Diodorus Siculus, tells us that Ammon, hard pressed by famine, took refuge in Crete, where he married Crētē, and became king of the island, which, formerly called Idæa, was afterwards called Crete. The Venetian name Candia may be either a corruption of Khandak,† a name given by the Arabs to a town built by them soon after their conquest of the

---

* According to others, he was a Cretan autochthon, or native of the soil.

† Or Khandax.

island in the early part of the ninth century, or may allude to the white appearance of its mountains as seen from the sea. The history of the Greeks or Hellenes begins upon the sea, and its commencement is the opening of intercourse between the islands and the coasts; but this commencement is marked by kidnapping and piratical expeditions, leading to reprisals, until at last every man's hand was raised against his fellow. To prevent the total destruction of the newly awakened forces, it was necessary to find a central point from which a new order of things might take its beginning, and this was found in Crete.

This island is situated between 34° 55′ and 35° 43′ N. lat., and 23° 30′ and 26° 20′ E. long. It is about a hundred and fifty miles in length, from Cape Corycus (now Cape Buso) in the west to Cape Sidero in the east; its average breadth is twenty miles. On the south it is washed by the Mediterranean, on the north by the sea of Candia; on the north-east are the straits of Scarpanto, which separate it from the island of that name, and on the north-west the straits of Cerigotto. Situated at an almost equal distance from Europe, Africa, and Asia, Crete was as it were the point of contact of these three continents, and the centre of the ancient world.

The island presents a very irregular outline, especially on the north coast, which is indented by deep gulfs, the chief of which are, from west to east, Kissamo, Canea,* Candia (on the site of the ancient Heraklion, called by the Greeks Megalo-Castro), Suda, an excellent roadstead, Armyro, Mirabella, and Sittia, and contains a large number of capes and promontories—Buso, Spada,

* More correctly, Khania.

Acrotiri, Retimo, Zuano, and Sidero. On the south side there is only one deep gulf, Messara, and three chief capes, Krio, Matala, and Langada. The island is traversed throughout its whole length by a lofty chain of mountains, composed of three distinct groups, which have from time immemorial formed the great natural or political divisions of the island. On the west, the Sphakiote mountains, the Leuka Orē of Strabo (modern Asprovouna—white mountains), so called from their retaining the snow on their summits through eight or nine months of the year. In the centre is Mount Psiloriti, the Mount Ida of the ancients, about eight thousand feet above the level of the sea. On the east, Mount Dicte, now Lassiti or Kittia. There are no important rivers in the island. The torrents which descend from the mountains dry up during the excessive heat ; but there are numerous springs on the lower slopes of the mountains, which abundantly supply the absence of irrigation. Although there are few trees upon the heights, the whole atmosphere of the island is said to have an aromatic odour arising from the flowers and shrubs which grow wild amongst the mountains, and furnish food for the hares and wild goats. No country in the world, perhaps, abounds more in natural excavations ; granite, schist, and slate are amongst the primary rocks.

The climate of Crete is mild and healthy ; the extremes of heat and cold are unknown. Observations taken during a whole year only showed a variation of 7°. In the height of summer, the heat is tempered by a breeze that blows from the north. The average temperature is 64° ; sometimes, however, the thermometer reaches 88° in summer. Snow falls on the mountains for two months of the year, and earthquakes are frequently felt in the north part of the island. The only endemic disorder known is leprosy. The soil is fertile, but since the wars of Greek Independence, agriculture has been neglected, and many parts of it remain uncultivated for want of labourers. Although the olive plantations have been in great part destroyed, and are greatly neglected, oil is still the staple production of the country. The vines produce famous wines, especially that of Malevisi ; fruits, flax, cotton, silk, and honey are the other most important productions. The lower slopes of the mountains are covered with oaks, chestnut trees, pines, walnut trees, myrtle, wild olives, and carob trees ; figs, oranges, and pomegranates are plentiful. The island abounds in slate. The goats of the island are a remarkably fine breed, and the sheep are highly esteemed.

Brandy, oil, fruits, honey, soap, and cheese are the principal articles of exportation. Silk is raised in small quantities, but of good quality. About two thousand tons of carobs are produced ; and oranges and lemons form a considerable article of export.

In ancient times the island was extremely populous ; the poets speak of it as containing a hundred cities, and we may reckon the number of its inhabitants to have been about 1,000,000. The inhabitants of Crete under the Venetians were estimated at about 250,000 souls. After the Turkish conquest the population was for a time greatly reduced, but afterwards gradually rose ; and at the time of the outbreak of the Greek Revolution in 1821, it reached 250,000, of whom about half were Mohammedans. At the close of the Revolution the inhabitants had dwindled down to 150,000, of whom 100,000 were Greek rayahs (or subjects), 25,000 Turks, and 25,000 Greeks from the Morea or the Ionian Islands. The cause of this decrease is to be found in the war carried on by the Cretans against both the Sultan and Mohammed Ali, and in the oppressive character of the Egyptian rule. Since then the population has again materially increased; Captain Spratt (*Travels and Researches in Crete*) calculated it as amounting to 210,000, less than 40,000 being Mohammedans. It is to be noticed that very few of these Mohammedans are Turks; they are almost entirely of native Cretan origin. The inhabitants, both Mohammedans and Christian, are, as a rule, tall and vigorous, and particularly skilful in the use of the bow, a reputation which they have maintained from ancient times. Amongst the Mohammedan part of the population are to be noted the Abadiotes, the descendants of the Saracens, who were expelled from the island by Nicephorus Phocas in the tenth century. They speak Arabic, and dwell in the neighbourhood of Mount Ida.

Although a brave and hardy race of men, ever ready to fight to the last for the recovery of their freedom and emancipation from Turkish rule, the Cretans, as a whole, seem to have preserved the national characteristics with which they have from time immemorial been credited. Travellers agree in describing them as ignorant, superstitious, and bigoted. In 1817 there were only three schools in the island. The Greek dialect spoken is very corrupt, but is the only language understood by the rural population. The *Kalóyeros*, or monk, like his

Russian *confrère*, is scarcely, if at all, superior to the peasant. Few of them can read, and, in fact, their chief claims to distinction lie in their wearing long beards, their vow of celibacy, and their conventual life in a monastery. The higher clergy can all read and write a little. The native Cretans are of the Greek Church, and are allowed the free exercise of their religion. The island is divided into eight bishoprics; the Bishop of Gortynia is appointed by the patriarch of Constantinople, and assumes the title of Archbishop. He wears a triple tiara, writes his signature in red ink, answers for all the debts of the clergy—a happy arrangement, hardly likely to suit his Anglican brethren—and nominates to all the vacant bishoprics in the island. He resides at Candia, and is the only Greek who possesses the privilege of entering that town on horseback.

The only important towns are: Candia (near the site of the ancient Cnossus), which was for a long time the capital of the island. It contains about fifteen thousand inhabitants. The houses are well built, but seldom rise above the height of two stories. The harbour is a mere basin formed by two moles, which project about two hundred and fifty yards into the sea. Canea (the ancient Cydonia), which has become the capital of the island since the renewal of the Turkish domination, a fortified town on the north-west coast, with eight thousand inhabitants; and Retimo (ancient Rhithymna), also on the north coast, a small fortified town with a good harbour. Ierapetra, on the south coast, on the site of the ancient Hierapytna, is a poor place, with a scanty population. The port of Suda, three miles from Canea, is the best in the island.

At the present time Crete forms part of Turkey, and

is under the government of a pasha, and is divided into three provinces, of which Canea, Retimo, and Candia are the capitals, these provinces being subdivided into twenty districts. The annual revenue from the island is reckoned at about £80,000; the rayahs pay a capitation tax, and other direct and indirect imposts. The garrison is about four thousand five hundred in number, consisting chiefly of Arabs and Albanians.

CHAPTER II.

ANCIENT CRETE, TO THE TIME OF ITS CONQUEST BY THE ROMANS.

IT is in Homer * that we first find mention of the ancient population of the island: "In the midst of the dark sea is a land called Crete, fair and fertile, surrounded by the waves; it contains ninety cities, and a vast number of inhabitants, who speak various languages—Achæans, stout-hearted Eteocretans (genuine Cretans), Cydonians, Dorians, and Pelasgians." The period to which Homer here refers was the reign of Minos, a half-mythical, half-historical personage, who is supposed to have been the first king of Crete. The earliest history of the island, like that of most parts of continental Greece, is so mixed up with mythology and fable that it is impossible to arrive at any clear conclusions concerning it. The Cretans themselves claimed that their island was the birthplace of Zeus (Jupiter), as well as the home of all the other divinities usually worshipped in Greece as the Olympian deities. Even when we come to Minos we are still far from being on firm ground. History is still legendary, and it is difficult to know how much is true amidst the mass of tradition by which his name is surrounded.

* *Odyssey*, xix. 172, 899.

Before the time of Minos, all interest was centred in the religious myths; the people were effaced by the gods; there were no indications of political life. With Minos the gods give place to the heroes, and he himself marks the transition between the two, belonging to the former by his birth and origin, and to the latter by his acts. The son of the god Zeus and the goddess Europa, he at the same time appears to us as the type of the ancient legislator and the founder of a great maritime power. Although we may not believe all that tradition tells us concerning his laws and adventures, it seems highly probable that he introduced a certain political order into Crete, and made the island powerful on sea; in fact, stripped of the marvellous, and reduced to his proper proportions, Minos remains the national hero and legislator of Crete. The inhabitants of the island, as given in the passage above quoted from Homer, differing as they did in origin, language, and religion, were further kept apart by the natural features of the island, as are its inhabitants at the present day. Crete has never attained political unity, it has always been divided amongst distinct groups of peoples, sometimes engaged in desperate internecine struggles. But it approached more nearly to such unity in the times of Minos, who, from his capital at Cnossus, exercised a certain amount of supremacy over the whole island, with the exception of the western portion, which maintained a kind of independence. This seems hinted at by the Greek historian Herodotus, who tells us that certain of the western inhabitants declined to take part in an expedition to avenge the death of Minos, as it had been an event in which they felt no interest.

The sea was the natural element of the Cretans; the situation of the island, with its extended coasts and numerous harbours, combined to attract them to it. Aristotle, in his *Politics*, says, "Nature seems to have placed the island of Crete in the most favourable position for holding sway over the rest of Greece, . . . on one side it is close to Peloponnesus, on the other it touches Asia. This admirable position gave Minos the Empire of the sea." There seems no doubt about the maritime supremacy of the island at some distant period. The impartial historian Thucydides remarks, "Of all the rulers of whom we have heard, Minos was the oldest possessor of a navy. He was master of the greater part of the sea which is now called Hellenic, he ruled over the Cyclades, and set up institutions in the greater part of these islands."

However, this naval supremacy was by no means attained without a struggle. At this time piracy and commerce went hand in hand, no disgrace at all being attached to the former, and the seas were utterly unsafe, being infested by corsairs. Most of the islands had become the haunts of brigands. Minos put an end to this state of things. He seems to have almost entirely driven the Phœnician pirates from the Ægean, but not the Carians, who afterwards appear closely united with the Cretans, and associated with their enterprises and colonies. We are told by Herodotus, that "in ancient times the Carians were the subjects of Minos, and went by the name of Leleges, dwelling among the isles and paying tribute to no man. . . . They served on board the ships of King Minos whenever he required."

The establishment of colonies in the time of Minos is

one of the principal events in the history of the Cretans. Hitherto confined within the limits of the island, they suddenly spread over the sea that surrounded them, and sent out in all directions colonies to the coasts of Asia Minor, the islands of the Ægean Sea, Greece, and even Italy, Miletus, Tenedos, Colophon, the islands of Chios and Rhodes, Delphi, and Taenarum in Laconia in Peloponnesus (the Morea).

But it was not only upon the coasts and islands of the Ægean that Cretan colonies were established. Minos undertook an expedition against Sicily, with the object of extending his empire over the western portion of the Mediterranean. According to tradition, Dædalus took refuge in this island from the wrath of Minos, and found an asylum with Cocalos, King of the Sicanians (Sicilians). Hearing this, Minos equipped a considerable fleet, and put in near Agrigentum, at a place which received from him the name of Minoa. After having disembarked his troops, he sent a message to the King, bidding him deliver up Dædalus. Cocalus, affecting readiness to deliver up the fugitive, and receiving Minos with apparent friendship, ordered a bath to be prepared for him by his three daughters, who, eager to protect Dædalus at any price, overheated the bath and drowned the Cretan king in the boiling water. According to another account, he died fighting against the Sicilians. Cocalus restored his body to the Cretans, and induced them to believe that Minos had met his death by accidentally falling into the bath. Not long afterwards Zeus instigated all the inhabitants of Crete (with the exception of the towns of Polichna and Præsus) to undertake an expedition against Camicus, the residence of Cocalus, for the purpose of avenging the death of Minos. They besieged Camicus in vain for five years, until they were compelled by famine to return. On their way along the coast of Iapygia, they were overtaken by a storm, which shattered their vessels. Being thus deprived of the means of returning to their native land, they remained where they were, and founded the town of Hyria. Thereafter they took the name of Iapygian-Messenians, and became inhabitants of the mainland in the place of islanders. This colony subsequently founded others, such as Brundusium. It also occupied Tarentum and its territory, for, when Phalanthus came to settle there with a band of Lacedæmonians, he was obliged to drive the Cretans from it. Part of the Iapygian colony left Southern Italy in consequence of internal dissensions, advanced along the Adriatic Sea, penetrated into Macedonia, and established itself in Bottiæis, so called from the leader of the band of emigrants. The Cretan name was for a long time preserved in Macedonia, for John Cantacuzene (a Byzantine emperor and historian) mentions a place called Cretensium, in the neighbourhood of Thessalonica, and consequently not far distant from the ancient Bottiæis.

The reign of Minos was the highest point of heroic royalty in Crete and of the power of the island; after him, both began to decline. According to tradition, Crete took a considerable part in the Trojan War, in which the Cretan Idomeneus even claimed to share the command of the Greek forces with Agamemnon. Although the Greeks assembled at Aulis rejected his claim, he nevertheless joined in the expedition at the head of his forces. "Idomeneus, famous with the spear, led the Cretans, and those who inhabited Cnossus and Gortys surrounded by walls, and Lyctus, and Miletus, and white Lycastus, and Phæstus, and Rhytium, populous cities, and the other dwellers in Crete, the island of a hundred cities."* According to one tradition, Idomeneus and Merion, the two grandsons of Minos, returned to their country after the Trojan War, and were buried with great honour, and venerated as national heroes. Another story is, that when Idomeneus set out on the expedition against Troy, he entrusted the administration of the kingdom to his adopted son, who slew his wife and daughter and seized the throne. Idomeneus, on his return, was obliged to take refuge on the coast of Calabria, where he founded Sallentum, which became the mother of several other colonies.

The Trojan War † produced the same effect upon Crete as upon all the other Greek states. One cause of the increasing weakness of Crete was, that it had discharged the best part of its population upon the coasts of Asia Minor ; a second cause was that, in the absence of its princes, the political bonds, which had more or less united its different peoples under the sway of Minos, became relaxed. During the troubles which followed the return of Idomeneus, after the fall of Troy, this bond was broken completely, and in Crete, as in the rest of Greece, royalty disappeared in the midst of general anarchy and confusion. In addition, plague and famine ravaged the island, and ended by depopulating it.

* Homer, *Iliad*, ii. 645.

† This is merely used as a convenient name, without the intention of vouching for the truth of the original story ; we are still in the unhistorical period.

Such was the situation of Crete when the Dorians, led by the Heraclidæ, or descendants of Hercules, invaded Peloponnesus (circa 1104 B.C.). This invasion caused a general movement of the Hellenic peoples, who left Greece and established themselves on the islands and neighbouring continents. Crete was naturally one of the first to receive the dispossessed inhabitants of Greece, who were in search of a new home.

The first of these colonies was founded under the leadership of Pollis and Delphus. It set out from the environs of Amyclæ in Laconia, where the Minyans, who had been driven from the islands of Lemnos and Imbros, had settled, revolted against the Dorians, and migrated anew from Laconia to Crete, accompanied by a number of Spartans, and made themselves masters of Gortyna and nearly the whole of the region of Dicte. Lyctus was the most important of their establishments, and was the great Dorian city.

A second expedition to Crete proceeded from Argos, in consequence of domestic feuds in the family of Temenus, the King of Argos. It was conducted by one Althæmenes, and consisted chiefly of those Dorian adventurers who, after the failure of their enterprise against Athia, found themselves without a home and without employment.

This colonization changed the aspect of the island. It became entirely Dorian. Its language, manners, political constitution, and social organization henceforth bore the impress of the Dorian race. This rapid transformation was materially assisted by the weakened condition of the island at the time of the arrival of the immigrants. The towns were almost deserted, and the population was exhausted by the calls that had been made upon it during the time of Minos and by subsequent internal dissensions.

From 1049 B.C. (circa) until 190 B C. the island remained Dorian ; but as the occupation had not been simultaneous, but spasmodic, the result was the formation of isolated settlements, which never united politically. Each colony with its own territory formed as it were a distinct separate state. This will in great measure account for the fact that, although, as Aristotle remarked, the situation of the island was most favourable for exercising a predominant influence over Greece generally, it sank to insignificance during historical times. From this time forth we hear little of it except as a recruiting-ground for mercenary soldiers, and a haunt of pirates. Beyond serving any one who was willing to pay them, the Cretans took no part in events taking place in other parts of Greece. When envoys from Greece came to ask aid from them against Xerxes, they sent messengers in the name of their state to the famous oracle of Delphi, and asked whether it would be well for them to lend assistance to the Greeks. "Fools!" replied the Pythoness, "do ye not still complain of the woes which the assisting of Menelaus, in the Trojan War, cost you at the hands of angry Minos? How wroth was he, when, in spite of their having lent you no aid towards avenging his death at Camicus, you helped them to avenge the carrying off by a barbarian of a woman from Sparta! When this answer was brought from Delphi to the Cretans, they thought no more of assisting the Greeks." *

* Herodotus, vii. 169 (Rawlinson's translation).

Again, they took no interest in the terrible struggle for supremacy between Ionian Athens and Dorian Sparta—the Peloponnesian War. They only appeared once, when, during the Sicilian expedition, they fought, although Dorians themselves, on the side of Athens. The Cretans took part in the war, not on the side of their own Dorian colony [Gela], but against it, not from choice, but simply in order to get money.[*]

The isolation of Crete from the Hellenic world continued ; and it is not until the last period of the political existence of the Greek peoples that we find her taking part in their affairs, during the intestine struggles in which Greece exhausted her remaining strength. At the commencement of the second century B.C., the island contained seventeen distinct settlements. Of these, Cnossus, Gortyna, Cydonia, and Lyctus were the most considerable, but none of them was sufficiently powerful to make itself master of the island. The whole island was divided into two camps. Polybius, the historian, gives the following description of the condition of things : " And indeed the whole island of Crete has lately been the scene of very great disorders, which were occasioned in the following manner. The Cnossians and Gortynians, having united their forces, had made themselves masters of the whole of Crete, with the exception of Lyctus. And when this single city still refused to submit, they resolved to conquer it by force, and to punish the inhabitants severely, that thus they might strike terror into the rest of Crete. At first all the people of the island took part in this enterprise, and turned their arms against the Lyctians. But, after some

* Thucydides, vii. 57.

time, discontent and jealousy, which had arisen—as was often the case amongst the Cretans, from small and inconsiderable causes—grew at last to an open and declared dissension, and broke the force of this confederacy. For the Polyrrhenians, the Ceretæ, the Lampæans, the Oreans, and the Arcadians separated themselves with one consent from their alliance with the Cnossians, and resolved to support the Lyctians. Among the Gortynians also, while the old men still firmly adhered to the Cnossians, the young men, on the other hand, contended with equal warmth in favour of the Lyctians. The Cnossians, becoming greatly alarmed by this sudden revolt of their chief allies, called in to their assistance a thousand mercenary soldiers from Ætolia. As soon as they arrived, the oldest of the Gortynians, having first gained possession of the citadel, and introduced the Cnossians and Ætolians into it, killed or drove out all the young men, and delivered their city to the Cnossians. Not long afterwards, when the Lyctians had led out all their forces, to make incursions into the territory of their enemies, the Cnossians, having received information of their absence, marched in haste and took possession of Lyctus, when it was left undefended. Having sent the women and children away to Cnossus, they set fire to the city, pillaged, and razed it to the ground. The Lyctians, on their return from their expedition, perceiving what had happened, were so struck with consternation and despair, that not one among them had the courage to set foot within the city. But when they had marched all round it, deploring with loud groans and lamentations the ruin of their country and their own unhappy fate, they retired and took refuge in the territory of the Lampæans, who received them with all the marks of friendship and affection: and having thus become, in a single day, strangers without laws or city instead of citizens, they continued afterwards to carry on the war against the Cnossians, in conjunction with the rest of the allies. Thus, in a most strange and astonishing manner, Lyctus, a colony from Lacedæmon, the most ancient city of the island, the inhabitants of which, descended from the Spartans, were confessed to be the bravest of all that were produced in Crete, was at once sunk and lost in irrecoverable ruin.

"The Polyrrhenians, Lampæans, and the rest of the allies, having considered that the Ætolians, from whom the Cnossians had received their mercenary forces, were at this time engaged in war against the Achæans and King Philip [of Macedonia], sent some deputies to these, to desire that they would enter into an alliance with them and send some troops to their assistance. To this request both Philip and the Achæans readily consented ; and, having received them into the general confederacy, they soon afterwards sent to their assistance four hundred Illyrians under the command of Plator, two hundred Achæans, and a hundred Phocæans. The Polyrrhenians, having obtained these successes, were now able to maintain the war with so great vigour, that they soon forced the Eleuthernæans, the Cydoniatæ, and the Apteræans, to keep close behind their walls, and at last compelled them to join their party and desert the alliance of the Cnossians. After this success, they sent in return to Philip and the Achæans, five hundred Cretans, as the Cnossians also, not long before, had sent a thousand of their troops to the Ætolians, to assist them severally in the war in which they were engaged. The young men likewise, who had been driven from Gortyna, having gained possession of the port of Phæstia, and afterwards of their own harbour also, maintained their posts with the greatest intrepidity, and from thence carried on the war again without intermission against the old Gortynians, who were masters of the city. Such was the state of affairs in Crete." *

Some time afterwards, the rival parties seem to have become reconciled, and to have both accepted the protection of Philip. But the Macedonian influence did not last long. Philip, when at war with the Rhodians, vainly solicited the aid of the Cretans. The latter subsequently made common cause with Nabis, the tyrant of Sparta, and admitted him to partnership in their piratical expeditions, and furnished him with mercenaries, who served as a body-guard.

In the mean time the island continued a prey to internal disorders. Apparently, however, attempts at political association were sometimes made. In the presence of common danger, when the island was threatened by an enemy from without, the inhabitants combined in a kind of federation, known as *syncretism*, although it is not known at what date it first came into existence. But no sooner was the danger past, than civil dissensions broke out afresh ; and, as it came to be recognized that national unity was impossible, partial associations were formed, consisting of the cities whose territories adjoined. But even these attempts at partial unification failed. The island, split up by its mountains, inhabited by a population which lacked national spirit or

* Polybius, iv. 5 (Hampton's translation).

any other feeling of combined interest, except defence against the attack of an enemy from without, was doomed to perpetual division in itself; and it was only in the last days of its independence that, for a brief period, it united against the Romans.

It has been said that the latter, who were then rapidly rising to the position of the greatest power in the world, attacked Crete for no other reason than a simple desire of conquering this celebrated island. But, besides this, there were other reasons. The conquest of Crete was necessary to the absolute dominion of Rome in Mediterranean waters ; and, in addition, it offered an excellent military position.

Excuses for attack were not wanting. During the course of their wars in the East, the Romans had met the Cretan bowmen on nearly every field of battle. Philip of Macedonia, and Nabis the tyrant of Sparta, had recruited their forces from these mercenaries. From that moment the fate of Crete was decided. In the treaty dictated by the victorious Flamininus to Nabis, it was stipulated that " he should not keep under subjection any city in the island of Crete, and that he should not enter into any alliance with the inhabitants." After the defeat of Antiochus, King of Syria, the Prætor Quintus Fabius Labeo undertook an expedition to Crete, and succeeded in securing the liberation of four thousand Roman prisoners, who were being kept there in the condition of slaves. Civil dissension was still raging upon the island, and in 184 B.C. an embassy was sent from Rome, with the object of reconciling the two rivals, the Cnossians and Gortynians. The Romans, who had again intervened in 174, now began to change their attitude, and, whereas they had formerly been content to play the part of mediators between the conflicting factions, commenced to assume an aïr of authority. In the year 170, during the war between the Romans and Perseus, King of Macedonia, it was found that the Cretans had furnished a larger number of mercenaries to Perseus than to the Romans. They thereupon hastened to send an embassy to Rome to make apologies, and received the reply that, if they desired to preserve the friendship of the Romans, they must without delay recall all their mercenaries who were serving under King Perseus. In 155 hostilities broke out between the Cretans and Rhodians, in which the latter do not seem to have had the advantage, since we are told by Polybius that they sent their admiral as an ambassador to request the intervention of the Romans, which was granted, and peace was concluded between the belligerents.

The state of anarchy on the island still continued, and the inhabitants had returned to their old profession of piracy. They made common cause with the Cilicians and other adventurers who infested the Mediterranean, and even furnished assistance to Mithridates, King of Pontus, against the Romans. To punish this insolence, as they regarded it, the Romans sent a fleet against Crete (71 B.C.). So confident was the commander of success, that he took more chains than arms on board with him. But he met with an unexpected reverse: the Cretans destroyed the greater part of his fleet, hung their prisoners to the yard-arm, and regained their harbours in triumph. This secured for the Cretans an honourable peace, but as it had been concluded by the prætor without the consent of the Senate and the people, the Romans refused to recognize it. The Cretans, understanding this, sent an embassy to Rome, with the request that the prisoners might be taken back and the old alliance re-established. They had almost obtained a favourable decree of the Senate, but Lentulus Spinther prevented its being carried into effect. In the end a decree was passed to the effect that the Cretan communities, if they wished to avoid war, should not only hand over the Roman deserters, but also the authors of the outrage perpetrated off Cydonia*—the leaders Lasthenes and Panares—for punishment; should deliver up all ships and boats of four or more oars ; should furnish four hundred hostages, and pay a fine of four thousand talents (£975,000). When the envoys declared that they were not empowered to enter into such terms, one of the consuls of the next year was appointed to depart for Crete, in order to receive satis-faction of the Roman demands or to begin war.

The Cretans thereupon held a council. The most prudent were in favour of submitting absolutely to the Senate ; but Lasthenes and Panares, who were afraid of being sent to Rome for punishment, stirred up the people to defend themselves by force of arms rather than submit to these excessive demands. Ac-cordingly, the Proconsul Quintus Metellus, on his arrival in Cretan waters, was met with a refusal. At Cydonia, where Metellus landed, an army of twenty-four thousand men was ready to meet him, and, after a desperate engagement, victory rested with the Romans. Metellus took possession of Cydonia, Cnossus, Lyctus,

* The defeat of the Prætor Marcus Antonius.

and other places. He treated the besieged with the utmost cruelty, who preferred to kill themselves rather than surrender to him. At last (67 B.C.), after a struggle which lasted two years, "Metellus became master of the whole island, and the last spot of free Greek soil thereby passed under the control of the dominant Romans; the Cretan communities, as they were the first of all Greek commonwealths to develop the free urban constitution and the dominion of the sea, were also to be the last of all those Greek maritime states that formerly filled the Mediterranean, to succumb to the Roman continental power." *

Although the political existence of Crete had been inglorious since the general disturbances caused by the Trojan War and the Dorian migrations, it at least distinguished itself at the last by a brave effort to retain its .independence; and its defeat, after a three years' resistance, was considered of sufficient importance to secure for its conqueror, Metellus, the surname of "Creticus," to commemorate his success.

* Mommsen, *History of Rome*, vol. iv. p. 353 (Eng. trans.).

CHAPTER III.

THE HISTORY OF CRETE, FROM THE TIME OF ITS CONQUEST BY THE ROMANS TO ITS CAPTURE BY THE TURKS.

THE island of Crete was now reduced to a Roman province, and united, for administrative purposes, with the district of Cyrenaica, or the Pentapolis, on the opposite coast of Africa—an arrangement which continued unchanged until the time of Constantine. From that time it was created a separate province under a governor of consular rank, and continued to form part of the Byzantine Empire until the ninth century.

Under Roman rule we hear of no events of importance connected with the island. It may be noted that Christianity early made its way there. St. Paul, on his journey to Rome, landed in Crete, effected some conversions, and left his disciple Titus to continue his work.

About 670 the Caliph Moawyah conceived the idea of the conquest of the Roman Empire, and a powerful expedition was sent to besiege Constantinople. While the greater part of his forces were employed against this city, Moawyah sent a division of his troops to invade Crete, which had already been visited by a Saracen army in 651. The island was compelled to pay tribute,

but the inhabitants were treated with mildness, as it was
the policy of the Caliph at this time to conciliate the
good opinion of the Christians, in order to pave the way
for future conquests. A few years later (678) peace was
concluded between the Caliph and the Roman Emperor.
In 715, during the reign of Anastasius, a celebrated
Arab chief ravaged the coasts of the island ; but it was
not until about the year 825 that the island came
definitely under Mussulman rule. During the reign of
Michael Balbus (the Stammerer) the island was left in
an unprotected state, owing to the disturbances which
had arisen consequent upon the rebellion of Thomas,
who had set himself up as a rival emperor to Michael.
In the year 815 about fifteen thousand Spanish Arabs
had been obliged to emigrate from Cordova, during the
reign of El Hakem, the Ommiade Caliph of Spain, and
settled in Alexandria. A band of these fugitives, taking
advantage of the situation, invaded the island, and
established a settlement upon it in 823. Shortly afterwards, the remainder of the Andalusian Arabs were
forced to quit Alexandria ; and, under the command of
Abou Hafs, who collected a fleet of forty vessels, they
ravaged the Cyclades, and joined their countrymen in
Crete. Delighted with the climate, and allured by the
fertility of the soil, they decided to settle permanently ;
it is said that the Mussulman leader, enchanted at the
aspect of the island, declared, on landing, that here at
last was the land "flowing with milk and honey" which
had been promised by Mohammed to the true believers.
The eminent historian, Mr. Finlay, remarking upon the
comparative ease with which Crete and Sicily fell into
the hands of Saracens, without offering any appreciable

D

resistance, considers it due to the fact that the change of rulers was welcomed by the inhabitants, who found the government of the Byzantine emperors more oppressive than that of their Arabian conquerors.

At first Abou Hafs confined himself to ravaging the island, and then returned to Spain for reinforcements. In the following year he returned, and, in order to make the settlement permanent, he burned his ships,* and constructed upon the coast a strong fortified camp surrounded by an immense ditch, from which it received the name of Khandax ; the town which was erected upon this site preserved this name, which was afterwards modified into *Candia*, and in course of time was bestowed upon the island itself. As the result of the conquest, Mohammedanism was everywhere established, the churches were converted into mosques, and the greater part of the ignorant population embraced the religion of the conquerors. When the rebellion of Thomas had been crushed, the Emperor Michael made an attempt to regain possession of Crete. An expedition was sent out under Photinus, commander of the armies of the East, and Damianus, *Comes Stabuli* (or Count of the Imperial Stables), but it was completely defeated. Damianus was slain, and Photinus made his escape with a single galley, to carry the news of the

---

* " When the invaders came down to the seashore, ready to embark with their plunder, they accused their general, who confessed that he had done this, of madness or treachery. ' Of what do you complain ? ' said he. ' I have brought you to a land flowing with milk and honey. Here is your true country ; repose from your toils, and forget the barren place of your nativity.' ' And our wives and children ? ' ' Your beauteous captives will supply the place of your wives, and in their embraces you will soon become the fathers of a new progeny.' "—Gibbon, ch. 52.

disaster to Constantinople. Basil, the Bishop of Crete, made good his escape to Constantinople, and exhorted the Emperor to do his utmost to prevent so important a possession passing into the hands of the infidels. Michael thereupon sent out a fresh expedition, consisting of seventy vessels of war, under the command of Craterus, the Governor of the Kibyrræot theme, or district. At first the Roman commander met with success, and, on landing, defeated the enemy in a desperate engagement. But he did not know how to take advantage of his victory. His soldiers abandoned themselves to rejoicings during the night, and, in the midst of the confusion, the Saracens invaded their camp, cut their troops to pieces, and captured the fleet. Craterus himself escaped in a merchant vessel, but was pursued and taken near Cos, where he was crucified by the Saracens. The island remained in the possession of the latter for a period of one hundred and thirty-five years, until the reign of Romanus II., when his general, Nicephorus Phocas, afterwards Emperor, drove them out of the island.

During this period Crete became a great slave-mart; and at this time the slave-trade was the most profitable branch of commerce in the Mediterranean. A large portion of the Greek inhabitants of Crete, having embraced Mohammedanism and established communications with the Christian slave-merchants in the Byzantine Empire, carried on a regular trade in purchasing Byzantine captives of wealthy families, and arranging exchanges of prisoners with their relations. A proverb, which occurs in the works of Constantine Porphyrogenitus, a literary Byzantine Emperor, shows the evil repute in which the island was held : "There are three abominable kappas (*i.e.* names commencing with the Greek K), Kappadocia, Kreta, and Kilikia." The Saracens undertook several piratical expeditions from Crete against various parts of the Byzantine Empire, in particular against Thrace, where they gained a decided victory near Thasos, during the reign of Theophilus, in the year 831. Ten years later, the Greeks made another attempt to recover the island, which proved equally unsuccessful. The Empress Theodora, mother of Michael III., sent out a numerous fleet with that object ; but while the commander Theoctistus was engaged in the siege of Candia, he suddenly left his army and withdrew to Constantinople. The troops suffered severely after they had been thus left to them-selves, and at length followed their general. At this period the Mussulman fleets were overrunning the Mediterranean. In 881, during the reign of the Emperor Basil, after the conquest of Syracuse, an Arab expedition left Crete, and, after having ravaged the islands of the Ægean, advanced as far as Proconnesus, in the Hellespont ; but their fleet was destroyed by the Greek admiral Nicetas with "Greek fire." In spite of this reverse, the Cretan Arabs put to sea with a fresh fleet, and ravaged the coasts of Peloponnesus. Nicetas hastened up, and, on his arrival at the port of Cenchreæ, the harbour of Corinth, was informed that the enemy were in the neighbourhood of Patras. Instead of going all round the peninsula, he transported his ships in a single night over the isthmus of Corinth, surprised the Saracens, and defeated them with great slaughter. The prisoners, especially the renegades, were treated with excessive cruelty. In 958 the Saracens again repelled an attack made upon the island of Crete during the reign of Constantine VII. (Porphyrogenitus). This attack was conducted by a worthless Paphlagonian named Constantine Gongyles, whose negligence and incapacity caused its total failure. However, the end of the rule of the Arabs was at hand: two years later, during the reign of Romanus II., Nicephorus Phocas, subsequently Emperor, and at the time one of the most capable generals of the Empire, resolved to wrest the island from its Mohammedan conquerors.

The injury inflicted on Byzantine commerce by the Saracen corsairs fitted out in the numerous ports on the north side of the island, compelled the inhabitants of many of the islands of the Archipelago to purchase protection from the rulers of Crete by the payment of a regular tribute. The trade of Constantinople and its supplies of provisions were constantly interrupted, yet several expeditions, fitted out on a large scale, had been defeated. Besides that undertaken during the reign of Constantine VII., the Emperor Leo had attempted (912) to put down Cretan piracy. A powerful army was assembled at Samos for the purpose of besieging Candia; but, after eight months, the expedition was defeated with great loss by the Saracens off the coast of that island.

The Emperor Romanus II., immediately on his accession to the throne, resolved to wipe out the disgrace of the defeat of Gongyles, to conquer the island of Crete, and expel the Saracen population. The latest victory of the Saracens had inspired them with greater audacity, and they continued to ravage the coasts with redoubled energy. Accordingly, when Nicephorus Phocas, who was commander of the army of the East, proposed to attack Crete, he was met with the most decided opposition, and the difficulties of the undertaking were exaggerated in every possible way. Attempts were also made to arouse the jealousy of the Emperor, by representing to him that his own reputation might be eclipsed by the glory which would accrue to Nicephorus, in case he met with success in carrying out so important an undertaking. However, he at last succeeded in obtaining the consent of the council to the expedition, and immediately set about making preparations, which were on a larger scale than anything that had hitherto been attempted, thereby showing how great was the terror inspired by the Cretan Saracens throughout the Empire, and how formidable a foe they were considered to be.

Troops were gathered together from Asia, Thrace, and Macedonia, together with Russian and Sclavonian mercenaries. A large fleet put to sea, accompanied by a number of "fire-ships," fitted with tubes for launching Greek fire, and transports loaded with provisions, engines of war, and arms of all kinds. Nicephorus set out in the month of July, and made for Phygela, near Ephesus, where the fleet was to assemble. Having learnt that the island was in a state of great alarm and disorder, consequent upon the news of his expedition, he immediately set sail for Crete, where he landed his forces without meeting with any opposition. At his first attack the Saracens fled, and Nicephorus marched straight upon Khandax (Candia), the capital of the island. When he came in sight of the town, he distributed his troops in different positions to blockade it, and sent out detachments in pursuit of those of the inhabitants who had fled for refuge into the mountains. They were discovered, and taken from their retreat, together with their cattle and belongings, to the Greek camp. Before leaving his ships, Nicephorus had taken the precaution of putting them in a place of safety, and had distributed them round the coast in such a manner as to intercept the supplies. His plan was to starve out the city, which was too strongly fortified to be taken without a regular siege; in the mean time he kept sending out detachments in all directions, which gradually effected the conquest of nearly the whole of the island during the siege of its capital.

Kurup, the Saracen Emir of Crete, shut up in the town, and despairing of breaking through a camp so strongly protected as that of Nicephorus, appealed for outside help to Africa and Spain. The two Caliphs, before complying with his request, sent persons to examine the state of affairs on the island. The unfavourable report which they took back to their masters —that the Greek fleet, which was very numerous and admirably posted, effectually cut off all access by sea, while the land forces were invincible—decided the latter to abandon the Cretans to their fate.

The fortress of Khandax itself appeared impregnable. On one side it was defended by the sea, on the other by an inaccessible rock on which it was built. The walls— built of sun-dried bricks, the mortar of which had been kneaded with the hair of goats and swine into a mass almost as hard as stone—were very high, wide enough for two chariots to drive abreast upon them, and surrounded by a double ditch. Nicephorus surrounded the place with a strong palisade, extending from one shore to the other, in order to cut off the besieged from all communication with the outside world.

It is related that Nicephorus, having heard that a force of forty thousand Arabs, who had taken up a position on a mountain in the interior of the island, intended to attack him whenever a favourable opportunity offered, himself took the initiative, surprised them one night when the moon was at its full, and cut them to pieces. The heads of the slain were cut off by his orders, carried back to the Greek camp in bags, and stuck upon the points of spears in sight of the ramparts, while others were cast into the place by means of catapults, that the besieged might realize the extent of their loss. During the winter Nicephorus occupied the time in drilling his soldiers, and preparing engines necessary to carry out the projected attack. The besieged already felt the pinch of hunger, while the besiegers themselves were not too well supplied with provisions, the stores which they had brought with them being almost exhausted. The soldiers, who felt the effects of the cold and rain, began to murmur, and demanded that they should be allowed to return home. Even the officers lost heart, and Nicephorus was only able to control them by sharing their labours himself. "Shall we show ourselves less courageous than our enemies?" he said to them. "They are suffering far greater hardships, without any hopes to sustain them. The Emperor is certain to send us fresh supplies. I have informed him of our need of them. Shall Christians, whom Heaven and earth protect, allow themselves to be outdone in patience by Saracens, who cannot expect assistance from either gods or men?" Encouraged by these words, they shouted, "We are ready to suffer all and to die with you." Shortly afterwards an abundant store of provisions for the besiegers arrived from Constantinople.

After a blockade of more than ten months, Nicephorus learned from deserters, who were continually flocking to his camp, that the majority of the inhabitants had died of starvation, and that the rest, reduced to desperate extremities, would be unable to resist an attack, although they had made up their minds to die rather than surrender. He thereupon decided to deliver the assault. On the 7th of May, at daybreak, he ordered his troops to take up arms, a breach was effected, and the place was taken by storm. Most of the defenders fell fighting; the survivors, who had taken refuge in flight, were pursued and massacred by the Greeks; some few threw themselves down from the top of the wall. Nicephorus ordered quarter to be given to those who laid down their arms. The city was full of booty, the accumulated wealth of piratical expeditions. The choicest part of this was reserved for the Emperor, while the soldiers were permitted to divide the rest. The fortifications of Khandax were razed to the ground, and a new fortress, called Temenos, was built on a high and inaccessible hill, and garrisoned by Armenian and Byzantine troops. The "fire-ships" were left in the harbour, to protect the fortress. After the complete subjugation of the island, Nicephorus returned to Constantinople with a rich booty and a large number of prisoners. He celebrated a triumph in the circus, amidst the acclamations of the people, who gazed with admiration upon the gold, silver, precious stuffs, carpets, jewels, gold-bedecked arms, and the throng of prisoners clad in white. The Emir Kurup and his son formed part of the triumphal procession.

During the hundred and fifty years of Mussulman rule in Crete, the islanders had embraced the religion of their conquerors. On the reconquest of the island, an Armenian monk, named Nicon, was sent thither by the Emperor, and succeeded in reconverting numbers of the inhabitants to Christianity. The conquest of Crete by Nicephorus Phocas replaced the island under Byzantine rule until the time of the Fourth Crusade (1204). In 1092, during the reign of Alexius Comnenus (the father of Anna Comnena, of whom we read in Sir Walter Scott's *Count Robert of Paris*), it revolted, owing to the oppression of the Byzantine administration. Two Cretans, Carycas and Rhapsomates, raised the standard of revolt, the one in Crete, the other in Cyprus, urging the inhabitants to declare themselves independent. John Dukas, the Empress's brother, set out for Crete, but on his arrival he found the island prepared to submit. The Cretan leader was deserted by his followers, and put to death as soon as the imperial fleet came in sight.

The Fourth Crusade never reached Palestine at all, but turned aside to take possession of the Byzantine Empire. The leader of these so-called Crusaders, Baldwin, Count of Flanders, was placed upon the throne of the East, and thus founded the Latin Empire of Constantinople, which lasted for fifty-six years. When the French and Venetians apportioned the Greek Empire, Crete was assigned to Boniface, Marquis of Montferrat, and King of Thessalonica. Boniface, however, had previously

entered into a private treaty with the Venetians to cede
to them all his possessions acquired by the Crusaders.
Pretending to have received a promise of the island of
Crete from the Emperor Alexis IV., he ceded both
Crete, Thessalonica, and his other territories to the
Venetians, who bound themselves to pay him the sum
of a thousand marks in silver, and to put him in
possession of territory in the Western part of the Empire
from their share of the partition, which should bring him
in a certain annual revenue.

Crete remained subject to the Venetians for more than
four hundred years. It was the most valuable possession that the great republic had acquired by the Fourth
Crusade, both on account of its commercial importance
and its position as a naval station. The Venetians,
however, were not destined to retain undisputed possession of it, although at first it submitted after one campaign. The Genoese, jealous of their rivals, but not
wishing to engage in open war against Venice, induced
Henry Count of Malta, a military adventurer, to put
himself at the head of the Cretan malcontents, and
secretly furnished him with assistance.

The first insurrection compelled the Duke of Candia,
as the Venetian governor was called, to re-embark.
The Republic sent out fresh troops, and the Count of
Malta abandoned the insurgents, and the Venetians
soon gained the upper hand. In order to familiarize the
islanders with their new owners, the Venetians sent
out considerable bodies of colonists at different periods;
and, by way of further securing the goodwill of the inhabitants, they confiscated half the insurgents' land, and
distributed it amongst the new settlers.

A second revolt soon broke out. The Governor of Crete summoned to his assistance the Prince of Naxos, a vassal of the Republic. The Prince responded to the call, but, disgusted at the haughty behaviour of the governor, he fomented a fresh insurrection, forced the governor to take refuge in his palace, and made himself master of the island. In spite of the despatch of fresh troops from Venice, the revolt still kept smouldering, and the Senate of the Republic recalled its governors one after the other, until at last one of them succeeded in establishing peace for a period of two years *

The system of continually changing the provincial governors naturally led to unsatisfactory results ; it did not allow time for repairing errors or successfully carrying out happily conceived reforms. The colonists had just reasons for complaint ; the governor was tempted to abuse a power which he knew he was not destined to retain for long, in order to make the most of his opportunity, while his subjects were equally ready to seize every chance of regaining their liberty.

In Crete, the brothers Cortazzi headed a revolt in 1242, in which the governor was killed. In 1243 another inhabitant of the island, Alexis Calergo, a man of rank

---

* P. Daru, in his *History of Venice*, gives fourteen insurrections of the Cretans between the years 1207 and 1365. In 1207, the revolt supported by the Count of Malta ; 1220, the revolt of the Agiostephanitæ ; 1226, a fresh insurrection ; 1228, revolt supported by John Vatatzes, Emperor of Nicæa ; 1242, revolt of George and Theodore Cortazzi ; 1243, eighteen years' revolt by Alexis Calergo ; 1324, three unimportant revolts ; 1324, revolt of Varda Calergo ; 1326, revolt of Leon Calergo ; 1327, insurrection put down by Giustinian Giustiniani ; 1341, revolt punished by Guistiniani and Morosini; 1361-4, revolt of the Venetian colonies ; 1365, revolt of the brothers Calergo, put down in the following year.

and influence, made preparations for obstinately resisting the conquerors. The Senate attempted to seize him, but he made good his escape, and the insurrection became a war, which lasted no less than eighteen years, and was carried on with varying success. At last, neither the Republic nor the island being unable to gain any decided advantage, negotiations were entered into. Calergo was granted various honours and privileges, and exemption from taxation, and was raised to the dignity of a Venetian nobleman. In order to make the peace, if possible, a lasting one, a fresh colony was sent into the island, which founded the town of Canea, on the site of the ancient Cydonia.

The Venetian system of colonization deserves attention. The island was divided into three parts: the first for the Republic, the second for the Church, the third for the colonists; the last portion was divided into 132 lots for the knights or nobles, and 405 for the foot soldiers. The distribution of the lots was not on equal terms: the larger were obliged to provide, in case of war, one horseman and two squires, with arms and horses; the others had to furnish ten foot soldiers. Later on, the colony was governed after the model of the mother city, by a duke or vice-doge and a grand council.

In 1361 the most important revolt broke out, which was not a revolt of the natives against the rule of their Venetian masters, but a general revolt of the colonists, the Venetian population of the island, who were highly indignant because none of the ancient families who had been transplanted from Venice into the colony were summoned to fill any of the magisterial offices of the Republic. They had demanded that twenty wise men

should be chosen from their number, who should represent them in the Great Council and look after their
interests. The question put to them by one of the
governors, "Are there any wise men amongst you?"
only served to irritate them still further. The different
way in which the Romans and Venetians treated their
colonies has been remarked upon as giving an explanation why the Roman colonies were so much more
attached to their mother country than the Venetians;
whereas the Romans granted their colonists fresh rights
as citizens of the mother city, the Venetians deprived of
their ancient privileges the citizens whom they sent to
Crete. On this occasion, the latter alleged as their
excuse for revolt the establishment of an impost, which
was to be levied for the repair of the harbour. They
took up arms, attacked the governor, threatened his life,
flung him into prison, together with his counsellors, and
chose as their leader one Gradenigo.

The rebels were so determined upon absolute separation from the mother Republic that they even abandoned
their allegiance to the Latin Church; they embraced the
Greek form of worship and doctrine, and substituted St.
Titus for St. Mark. Meanwhile, the whole population
was supplied with arms, the prisons were flung open, and
the indiscriminate aid of the criminal classes solicited;
those who ventured to disapprove of the insurrection
were massacred.

The Republic acted feebly at first. Three commis-
sioners were sent to exhort the rebels to return to their
allegiance, but they were not allowed to land, and finally
were forced by threats to return.

Next, five other deputies were sent, but met with an

even more insulting reception. They were allowed to land, and conducted before the governor of the island, through the midst of large bodies of soldiers and an excited population, which pursued them with jeers and hooting. Such a reception was not likely to lead to any favourable result.

On the return of the embassy, the Republic, despairing of bringing back the Cretans to allegiance by persuasion, wrote to the Italian powers, the kings of France and Naples, and the Greek Emperor, begging that they would not render any assistance to the rebels. Even after the required promise had been given, some members of the council were in favour of simply blockading the island, instead of attacking it.

One of the causes of the apparent feebleness and unwillingness to act displayed by the Venetians was the lack of men from which to recruit her army, her population having been exhausted by two serious wars. She was accordingly obliged to have recourse to the mercenary soldiers of fortune, who traversed all parts of Europe where war was going on, ready to sell their services to the highest bidders.

The expedition was not got ready until 1364. Its commander was a Veronese captain named Luchino dal Verme, who was at the time commander of the troops of the Duke of Milan ; and on the 10th of April a fleet of thirty-three galleys set out, with six thousand men on board. The insurgents had failed to make the best use of the time during which they had been left unmolested. They had assassinated a number of the islanders who were suspected of preferring Venetian rule, and their leader himself did not escape their fury. A certain party was in favour of handing over the island to the authority of the Genoese; but the latter, being in the throes of civil dissension, did not venture to recommence war against the Venetians.

The army disembarked, without meeting any resistance, on the 7th of May. On the 10th dal Verme set out on his march, forced the passage of a defile in which the islanders were posted, and made his way to the gates of the capital, the outskirts of which he burned, while at the same time the fleet made its appearance at the entrance of the harbour. The rebels were surprised by this vigorous attack, and were unable to resist the assault. They sent deputies to Michieli (the Venetian admiral) to implore forgiveness. The admiral ordered the gates to be thrown open, took possession of the harbour, and entered the capital with his troops, who immediately proceeded to the work of plundering it.

Some of the rebels perished on the scaffold, some made good their escape to the neighbouring islands, and others fled to the mountain fastnesses. The conquest of the island had only lasted three days; the news was received at Venice with manifestations of delight, and celebrated by public festivities.

We now come to the last revolt, which broke out as early as the following year (1365). The rebels, under the command of three brothers belonging to the distinguished family of Calengo, instead of attempting to gain possession of the capital, fortified all the easily defensible strongholds of the island, and established themselves in positions where it would be difficult for the Venetians to attack them. In 1366, after a desperate struggle, victory remained with the Republic; nearly all the chief movers in the insurrection were put to death ; even the wife and children of the leaders were not spared. The following extract from a letter from Paolo Loredano to the Doge showed the stringent measures which were taken to prevent the possibility of any future outbreak : "The rebels have no longer any leaders ; terrible examples have been made in order to frighten those who might be inclined to put themselves at their head. Their strongholds and fortresses, which we have not thought it desirable to occupy ourselves, have been razed to the ground ; the inhabitants have been removed elsewhere. The surrounding country will remain uncultivated ; it is prohibited, under pain of death, even to approach it. All regulations tending to keep up the pride or the spirit of independence of the colonists have been abolished. The native inhabitants will have no further share in the administration or public magistracies, and their obedience to you will be guaranteed by the close watch kept over them by your faithful representatives."

For about the next three hundred years the island re-mained peaceful, if not contented, under Venetian rule. The government of Crete by the Venetian oligarchy was, like that of their other dependencies, very arbitrary and oppressive, and, as we have seen, numerous in-surrections were the result. But, with all its defects, their administration did much to promote the material prosperity of the country, and to encourage commerce and industry ; and it is probable that the island enjoyed during this period greater prosperity than at any subse-quent time. Their Venetian masters at least secured to the island external tranquillity, and it is singular that the Turks were content to leave them in undisturbed possession for nearly two hundred years after the capture of Constantinople.

We now approach the critical period in the history of the island.

Up to the middle of the seventeenth century, Crete had resisted all the intermittent attempts of the Ottoman Turks to gain possession of it. It was at this period that the Ottoman Empire reached its greatest geographical extent: with the exception of Podolia, which was ceded to the Turks by Poland, Crete was their last European acquisition. We will now proceed to give an account of the Turkish attack upon Crete, and of the siege of Candia, one of the most memorable in history, as it was certainly the longest. The town did not fall until it had sustained a war of twenty-five years, a blockade of thirteen years, and a siege, during which the trenches remained open for two years, three months, and twenty-eight days.

At this time the occupant of the Ottoman throne was Ibrahim, a vicious and feeble ruler; but his vizier, Mohammed Pasha, was an able and enterprising man, and it was his ambition that inspired him with the idea of depriving the Venetians of the island. The following was the alleged cause of hostilities. In the year 1644 some Maltese galleys seized a Turkish vessel which had been despatched by the Sultan to Mecca, and a fleet of merchantmen which was on its way to Cairo. There were on board the Sultan's vessel one of his favourite sultanas, and a son whom she had borne him. In spite of remonstrances, the Maltese not only refused to surrender the captives, but anchored off the coast of Candia;

subsequently, the captives were taken to Malta, where the mother died of grief, and the boy was handed over to the monks, and became a Dominican. This incident enraged the Sultan, who held the Venetians, as masters of the island, responsible for what had taken place. The Vizier Mohammed took advantage of his master's rage to propose to him, not the destruction of Malta, upon which the Turks had already made an unsuccessful attempt, but the conquest of Crete, the possession of which they had long eagerly desired. This island was nearly all that remained to the Venetians of the divided Empire of the East; after more than twenty revolts, it had at length submitted, and was, if not contented, at least peaceful; in any case, they could hardly have desired to exchange the rule of the Venetians for that of the Turks.

The latter, well aware of the difficulties of the enterprise which they were undertaking, made elaborate preparations to ensure its success, and assembled a large army and fleet. The Venetians, alarmed at this, demanded an explanation; but the Porte reassured them, by declaring that they were merely intended to threaten the Order of Malta.* The Venetians, not being completely satisfied with these protestations, equipped a squadron of twenty-three galleys at Candia, and called out and drilled the militia, who had become disorganized owing to long-continued peace. However, all doubts as to the object of the Turkish preparations was soon set at rest; the Sultan declared that the expedition was intended for Malta, and in March, 1645, the fleet,

* At this time Malta was in the possession of the Order of the Knights of St. John of Jerusalem.

consisting of 348 vessels of war, left the Dardanelles, accompanied by a large number of transports, with 50,000 men on board.   When the Grand Vizier thought the fleet was not far from Crete, he caused the *baile*, or ambassador, of Venice to be arrested at Constantinople, and gave him a detailed list of grievances which the Porte declared it had against Venice.   This arrest was not known at the latter place when, on the 24th of June, the news arrived that the 50,000 Turks, under the command of Yussuf, had landed on the west of the island, near Canea, and, immediately after disembarking, had taken possession of the fortified position called St. Theodora.   The Turkish general established his head-quarters at Casal Galata, and proceeded to lay siege to Canea, into which the governor had hastily thrown a few thousand men.

At this time there were several fortified points on the island, all on the north side : Grabusa, some strongholds on the islands off the extreme west of Crete ; Canea ; and, close to the latter place, at the bottom of a deep bay, Suda, where the Venetian fleet was assembled, under the command of Antonio Capello. Further towards the east was Retimo ; then Candia, the capital of the island, and the residence of the governor, Antonio Cornaro.   Opposite Candia was the little island of Standia,* which afforded good anchorage for large ships.   To the east of Candia was the fortress of Spina Longa, on the extremity of a cape, jutting far out into the sea.   Lastly, at the eastern extremity of the island, was the strong position of Sittia.

The Venetians were thrown into a state of great

* A contraction of *Es tan* (*ten*) *Dia.*

consternation at the news of the Turkish attack, and were especially indignant at having been deceived. They made great efforts to save the island ; the clergy gave up part of their revenues, and patrician dignities were bestowed upon simple citizens on payment of sums of money. A pressing appeal was sent to all the Catholic powers to ask their assistance, but it did not meet with a very hearty response. The Pope, the Grand Duke of Tuscany, and the Order of Malta furnished a fleet of twenty galleys ; France secretly offered a subsidy of 100,000 crowns, and Spain confined herself to lavish promises. In the mean time, while the Venetians were occupied with these preparations, Canea had capitulated, after a siege of fifty-seven days, during which the inhabitants had defended themselves with the greatest courage. This success gave the Turks the command of a harbour, and a headquarters for their troops. In 1646 Retimo was carried by assault. In 1648, after having gained a firm footing on the island, they laid siege to Suda, before the gates of which they had erected pyramids made of the heads of 5000 Christians, and commenced the siege of Candia ; a line of circumvallation was drawn round the place, and the trenches were opened.

Then commenced a succession of assaults, sallies, and cannonades unexampled in history. The repeated attacks were resisted with the utmost bravery by the inhabitants, under the leadership of Morosini. For more than twenty years the struggle continued with varying success, both on land and sea ; but the Venetians, in spite of their maritime superiority, were unable to prevent the Turks from sending assistance to the besiegers.

Towards the end of 1666, the Grand Vizier, a man of great energy and activity, arrived on the spot, with the intention of personally directing operations. With an army of 80,000 men, on the 22nd of May in the following year, he established his headquarters close to Candia, the garrison of which consisted of only 10,000 soldiers, under the command of Francesco Morosini, and the flower of the Venetian nobles. From the 23rd of May to the 18th of November thirty-two assaults and seventeen sorties took place, during which the garrison lost about 4000 officers and men, the Turks more than 20,000. In May, 1668, the Marquis de Ville, commander of the infantry of the defenders, was replaced by the Marquis de Saint André Montbrun, whom the Venetians had selected with the object of flattering Louis XIV., king of France, and inducing him to take an active part in the defence of Crete. The result was that Louis sent some money to the Venetians, and allowed them to levy troops in France. Inspired by his example, the Pope and the knights of Malta sent assistance, while the forces of the Venetians were largely increased by volunteers, amongst them the Duc de la Feuillade, who led out 500 men of high birth, and paid all their expenses out of his own purse.

The campaign, which had by this time cost the Turks 23,000 men, had exhausted the Venetians. At the pressing entreaties of the Venetian ambassador, Louis XIV. was roused to greater interest in the affairs of Crete, and promised to send a considerable number of reinforcements, amounting to 6000 men, under the command of the Duc de Beaufort and the Duc de Navailles ; but when the fleet appeared off the coast of

the island, on the 6th of June, 1669, Candia was almost
at the end of its resistance. Unfortunately, again,
although the arrival of the French troops revived, in
some measure, the failing hopes of the defenders, the
new-comers were inclined to rashness, and unwilling to
listen to the more prudent counsels of Morosini. Much
against his will, the latter consented to a general sally,
the result of which proved disastrous. The defenders
lost 500 men, and, what was worse, the ill-success of
the sortie caused dissensions amongst the defenders.
An unsuccessful attempt at a bombardment of the
enemy's camp, and the blowing-up of a French warship,
induced the admiral, the Duc de Navailles, to return in
disgust to France, which led to the withdrawal of the
remainder of the naval forces which had hitherto been
assisting the Venetians, together with the volunteers,
and the besieged found themselves reduced to a force
of 3000 men. The Turks delivered a general assault,
and Morosini, seeing that the idea of further resistance
was hopeless, offered to capitulate. The Grand Vizier
eagerly accepted the proposal, and, respecting the heroic
resistance that had been offered by the garrison, granted
them honourable conditions, in no wise dishonourable
for the Republic.

The capitulation was signed on the 6th of December,
1669. It was agreed that the Venetians should abandon
Candia within twelve days; the inhabitants were to be
at liberty to take their belongings and follow the
garrison. The island itself was to be ceded to Turkey,
the Venetians being allowed to keep three ports—
Grabusa, Spina Longa, Suda, and the dependent
islands. In exchange for this, the Republic was to retain

possession of its conquests in Bosnia and Dalmatia. The treaty was received with disapproval at Venice, but was ratified, since it was felt that it was impossible to continue the war. Morosini was accused in the Senate of having entered into negotiations with the Turks without having previously been authorized to do so, and would probably have been condemned had not his services been required elsewhere. Venice did not long retain possession of the points on the island that had been left to her by the treaty ; before the end of the seventeenth century Grabusa was handed over to the Turks by the treachery of the governor, who accepted a bribe of a thousand sequins ; and in the commencement of the following century, by special arrangement, Suda and Spina Longa were abandoned.

Thus Venice lost possession of Crete, after having had possession of it for nearly five centuries. Its government had been modelled on that of the Republic. The island was governed by a proveditor-general from Venice, who had under him the four proveditors of Canea, Candia, Retimo, and Sittia. For judicial matters there were Rettori, or judges, also sent from Venice, each of whom was assisted by two counsellors, who were natives of the island. The municipal administration was in the hands of the Cretans ; taxes were very moderate. The native nobility enjoyed feudal privileges, and were bound to have a certain number of militia from among their vassals and tenants ready when called. As already mentioned, the period of Venetian rule was probably the period during which the island enjoyed the greatest prosperity ; agriculture was encouraged, the island supplied Venice with corn, and its commerce was important and profitable.

CHAPTER IV.

THE HISTORY OF THE ISLAND, FROM ITS CAPTURE BY THE TURKS TO THE PRESENT TIME.

IF the inhabitants of Crete had chafed under the government of the Venetian Republic, they soon found that they had not profited by the exchange of masters. Several attempts to shake off Turkish rule were repressed with pitiless severity, and the people were handed over to the tender mercies of an insubordinate soldiery, who sometimes rose even against their own commanders. Thus we learn that, in 1688, Soul Fikar Pasha, the governor of the island, was massacred by his own soldiers. The pashas do not appear to have made any attempts to restrain the excesses of the Turkish troops, but rather to have encouraged them ; besides, the governorship of the island, being one of the most important and lucrative of the Turkish possessions, was generally bestowed upon one of the Sultan's favourites, who extorted as much as he could from the unfortunate inhabitants. It is true that the Porte sometimes could not help punishing those whose cruelties and exactions went beyond all bounds : thus, in 1728, in the reign of Ahmed III., the defterdar * of the island, not content

* A title formerly given to a kind of finance minister.

with having disorganized the system of rents, had forged four firmans, or imperial rescripts, counterfeited the official signatures, and even that of the Sultan. For these offences he was put to death. But, even if a high official was now and again punished, the Mussulmans individually exercised a tyranny over the inhabitants of the island that was almost unbearable. They carried off at pleasure the daughters of Greek households who had taken their fancy, and the injured parents had no redress. Even as late as the end of the eighteenth century, no Greek, with the exception of the archbishop, was allowed to enter any of the towns on horseback. The Bishop of Canea on one occasion ventured to do so; the janissaries who were on guard at the gate called the soldiers together, related what had taken place, and decided to burn the bishop and all the priests. They were on the point of carrying out their purpose, when the pasha intervened, and appeased the excited soldiery by publishing an edict forbidding any Greek to pass the night within the walls of Canea; only the women were allowed to remain. The result of the Turkish oppression was, that the cultivation of the soil was abandoned, commerce was at a standstill, and poverty prevailed throughout the island; the inhabitants, forced to support life by a diet of olives, salt fish, and cheese, were attacked by leprosy, which for a period of eighteen months claimed hundreds of victims.

A few words may be added as to the Turkish administration introduced into the island after its conquest. It was divided into three districts, under three pashas, who resided at Candia, Canea, and Retimo. The first took precedence of the other two:

he was inspector of the forts and arsenals, and appointed the beys who were charged with the care of the different strongholds of the island. The pasha's counsellors consisted of a kiaya, or general administrator of affairs; the agha of the janissaries, captain of the troops and head of the police; two artillery officers; a defterdar; and an officer whose duty it was to guard the imperial treasury. The legal authorities were the mufti, whose office it was to lay down the law on all cases submitted to him, and the kadi: the former interpreted the laws dealing with the division of property, rights of inheritance, and marriages; while the kadi received the declarations and complaints of those who considered themselves aggrieved, and decided between plaintiff and defendant. In 1785 the Turkish garrisons of these three places amounted to about 15,000 men; the Mussulman population of the island was nearly 200,000; the Greek, the number of which diminished nearly every year, not more than 150,000: whereas, in its prosperous times, the inhabitants had numbered more than 1,000,000. The taxes imposed upon the Christians were of two kinds—one-seventh of the product of the soil, and the kharaj, or capitation-tax, paid by all male Christians above sixteen years of age; this tax was equivalent to about thirteen shillings. The land-tax could be paid in kind,—in corn, flax, or cotton. A tax was imposed upon silk. The following was the ecclesiastical government of the island: the Patriarch of Constantinople nominated the archbishop, who in turn nominated the bishops, who appointed the parish priests. The archbishop, in addition to the revenues of his diocese, received every year a certain sum from the bishops, who in turn exacted a tax from the Christian families, in order to pay the archbishop's tribute to the Sultan. The income of the bishops was made up partly by voluntary contributions, and a fee was paid for every celebration of marriage. The numerous religious taxes, and those established by the Turks, caused a large number of Christians to renounce their religion, and the traveller Pococke informs us that, a hundred and twenty years after the Turkish conquest, on the occasion of his visit to the island, the number of renegades was very considerable.

At the commencement of the nineteenth century, the Turkish oppression in Crete reached its height. The island had hitherto remained faithful to the Sultan, and had manifested no desire to imitate their countrymen in the Morea,* where revolt had broken out (1821). Embassies from various parts of Greece did not succeed in rousing the Cretans to an attempt to shake off the yoke, although they were even worse off than the Christian subjects of Turkey on the mainland. This seems somewhat surprising; it would appear that the oppression from which they had suffered had made them apathetic, and led them to underrate their strength.

A Greek enjoyed no civil rights in the island. If he were a landowner, he was deprived of his income by the governor, or even by any Turk who happened to be his neighbour, and he had no redress or right to complain. If he had ventured to summon his spoiler before a legal tribunal, he would not even have gained a hearing; in any case, it was not worth his while to do so, as it meant the destruction of himself and his

* See next chapter.

family; accordingly, there was nothing left for him but to suffer in silence. A Turk who wanted money had recourse to a very simple expedient for procuring it : he went into the first Greek shop he came to, and demanded from the proprietor the payment of the money which he had lent him a year ago. In the majority of cases, the shopkeeper had never seen his pretended creditor before; but he was obliged to hand over the money, since refusal would probably have meant death.

Four or five years before the outbreak of the revolution, all the Turks throughout the Empire had been ordered by the Sultan to give up the practice of carrying arms. All regretfully submitted, with the exception of the Cretans, who continued to carry their yataghans and fire-arms, the authorities of the island being afraid to employ force to compel their obedience. The Cretan Mussulmans—the sons of Greek women by Turkish fathers—were the most bitter persecutors of the Greeks. The papádes, or priests, were in particular the object of their attacks. When they met an unoffending ecclesiastic, it was a common thing for them to fire upon him, by way of testing their aim ; and the Greeks of the quarter were obliged to pay a certain sum, before they were allowed to take up the corpse. This was called "the law of blood," and the amount thereby raised was handed over to the chief mosques. When a Greek was executed, the sentence was carried out in any place that the authorities considered suitable. After the criminal's head had been cut off, all the Greeks of the neighbourhood were obliged to subscribe a large sum, in order to procure the removal of the headless trunk from their midst.

When a man was condemned to be hanged, the punish-ment was carried out at the door of a shop—a grocer's being generally chosen, as being most frequented by customers—and the unhappy proprietor was obliged to spend three days with the body under his nose, and was unable to get rid of it without disbursing a considerable amount.

We have mentioned the ruling Turks and the subject Greeks as constituting the two main divisions of the population of the island ; we must now mention a separate class, who had for a long time resisted all attempts to bring them into subjection, even during the period of Venetian rule. The hardy mountaineers of the north-west part of the island retired into the gorges of the long chain of mountains terminating in Capes Buso and Spada, which from the snow on its heights was called the " White Mountains," and for more than a century resisted the attacks of the Venetians. They were called Sphakiotes, from Sphakia, the chief township. Even when the Venetians sent out their colony, of which we have already spoken, they refused to consort with the new arrivals, and avoided all contact with the Venetians, as they had formerly avoided the Greeks and Saracens. At last, their resist-ance ceased, and they were left in peace ; but they continued to carry on the practice of piracy, with the authorization of the Venetian magistrates, who con-tented themselves with exercising a general supervision over them, and treated them with the greatest con-sideration.

The Turkish rule did not bring about any change in their position or manner of life ; they continued to live in the mountains, speaking a dialect more related to the primitive language than that of the rest of the inhabitants, supporting themselves by piracy, hunting, and the sale of milk-cheeses. For a long time they were the most skilful archers on the island, and later they showed themselves equally skilful in the use of the gun. At the end of the eighteenth century, travellers relate that they still kept up the Pyrrhic dance, a mimic war-dance, representing attack and defence in battle, the origin of which is traced back to the Dorian inhabitants of the island. For a long time the Sphakiotes escaped the kharaj; but about 1770 the Mussulmans attacked them, on the pretence that they intended to hand over the island to the Russians. They would doubtless have offered as effectual a resistance as they had hitherto done, had not some of the younger Sphakiotes been induced by bribes to lead the enemy over the mountains. The Sphakiotes were surprised; a number of villages were destroyed, a number of the inhabitants massacred, and the women and children carried off and sold as slaves.

We have noticed the apparent apathy of the Cretans at the outbreak of the Greek Revolution, and their lack of eagerness to respond to the invitation of their fellow-subjects on the mainland. In the month of June, 1821, however, they began to rouse themselves. During this month, the Cretan Turks, the most desperate villains in the Empire, who inhabited the strongholds of the northern part of the island, had assassinated a large number of Christians, hanged several dignitaries of the Church, and profaned the churches; and, on the 24th of June, after a general massacre of the Greeks at Canea, they thought themselves strong enough to demand that all the inhabitants of the south of the island should lay down their arms. This demand irritated the Sphakiote mountaineers, who, although they had paid tribute to the Porte since the disaster of 1770, had never looked upon themselves as its subjects. Accordingly, as soon as the Sphakiote chiefs heard of the intentions of the Turks, they sent a deputation to their neighbours, the Abadiotes, in order to induce them to sink all petty differences, and make common cause with them against the Turks.

The Abadiotes were descended from a military colony, which had been sent by the Saracens to Crete in the ninth century, under the leadership of a sheikh named Abadia, and preserved the primitive religion of Mohammed, which is a pure deism. However, as it is probable that the new converts to Mohammedanism did not at once renounce Sabeanism,* many traces were to be found among the Abadiotes of the ancient worship of the stars. They were similar in appearance to the Bedouins, with their tawny skin, beautiful teeth, brilliant, deep-sunken eyes, and slender form. When the Sphakiote deputies informed them of the object of their mission, they swore to forget the past, and to join the Sphakiotes against the Turks. Meanwhile, the Sphakiotes, not feeling sure about the issue of their negotiations with the Abadiotes, gave the following reply to the Pasha of Canea, who demanded that they should lay down their arms. They pointed out the necessity, under which they were, of being continually on their guard, so as to be able to defend

* The worship of the fire, sun, and stars.

themselves and their flocks from the attacks of wild beasts ; and, finally, while renewing their oath of sub-mission to the Porte, and swearing that they were ready to fight for the Sultan against the insurgents, they insisted that it was an absolute necessity for them to retain their arms. This reply enraged the pasha, who sent a fresh message to the Sphakiotes to the effect that, if they did not lay down their arms at once, they would be treated as enemies and rebels. The Sphakiotes returned the following answer : " Since the Mussulmans do not believe our promises, and are asking for our arms in order that they may afterwards have our heads, let them come and take them."

The Sphakiotes, together with the Abadiotes, de-scended into the plain, in number about nine hundred. The Turks marched out to meet them, but were defeated and obliged to retreat and shut themselves up in Canea. As soon as the insurrection of the Sphakiotes became known, the whole island raised the standard of the Cross, and took up arms. Courmoules, a Cretan of noble family, a pretended convert to Mohammedanism, tore off his turban, proclaimed himself a Christian, and put himself at the head of the insurgents of Retimo. The Turks were everywhere defeated in the open field, and obliged to shut themselves up in their strongholds. In less than a month, the Cretans were masters of nearly the whole island, and the pashas were blockaded in Candia, Canea, and Retimo.

These results were partly due to the energy and courage of a young Cretan named Antonios Melidones, who, as soon as he heard of the rising in Crete, had hastened from Asia Minor at the head of all the Cretans

F

who were scattered about that part of the world. Emboldened by the first success of the insurrection, he conceived the idea of making his way through the northern part of Crete, which was still guarded by the Turks, and, obliging the enemy to retire to the shelter of their fortresses, various places fell into his hands. On one occasion, he was surprised and surrounded by the army of the Pasha of Megalo Castro ; * in an instant he put himself at the head of his men, routed and pursued them back to the fortress. On the following day a Turkish detachment which ventured to leave it was cut to pieces. The pasha, struck with admiration at the gallant exploits of the young Cretan, sent a message to him, expressing a wish to see him. The reply was, " In a few days you will be a prisoner in my tent, and then you will have an opportunity of examining me at your leisure."

The increasing reputation of Melidones aroused the envy of Roussos, chief of the Sphakiotes. Desiring to get his rival out of the way, the latter sent a message to Melidones that a division of the enemy's forces was encamped at Abadia. He reckoned upon the rashness of Melidones and the superior numbers of the enemy to ensure his destruction ; but Melidones laid his plans so well that, although he only had three hundred men at his command, he gained a decisive victory, and brought back a large booty consisting of stores of biscuits and powder. This only increased the animosity of Roussos ; he invited his rival to dinner, and the latter, suspecting nothing, accepted the invitation. The Sphakiote leader took the opportunity of insulting him, and accusing him of ulterior motives ; but Melidones, in a few dignified

* Candia.

words, completely justified himself, and left the table amidst the applause of the Sphakiotes themselves, who declared themselves ready to fight and die for him. Roussos, enraged at the turn events had taken, pretended to desire a reconciliation, invited Melidones to an interview, and treacherously slew him.

The assassination of Melidones was a great blow to the insurgent cause. Roussos, although a brave soldier, was by no means a competent general. Under these circumstances, an appeal was made to headquarters, and Michael Comnenus Afendallos was sent from the Morea to take his place. This officer, who was of unprepossessing appearance, proved incapable. He drew up a military code and a form of oath, and addressed several proclamations to the people; but he took no decisive measures, and thus allowed the enemy, who were still blockaded in their strongholds, time to recover. Full of ambitious ideas, and claiming descent from the ancient royal family of the Comneni, members of which had formerly occupied the throne of the Byzantine Empire, he arrogated to himself the position of viceroy of Crete, and expressed his intention of claiming the taxes and tribute paid by the islanders and Sphakiotes to the Government of Constantinople. Such conduct did not tend to increase the popularity of Afendallos, and the Sphakiote chiefs demanded that he should be superseded. His place was taken by a French officer of distinction, and an ardent supporter of the Greeks, named Baleste, who arrived on the island, accompanied by a number of enthusiasts. Baleste, on his arrival, learning that the Turks were fitting out a fleet at Alexandria, intended to carry on operations against Crete, carried on the siege of Canea with increased vigour, defeated the Pasha of Retimo, and forced him to shut himself up in the town.   On the 27th of April, 1822, he defeated the Turks both on land and sea.   In the middle of May, the Egyptian fleet landed twelve thousand Turks on the island.   Baleste united all his forces, and advanced to meet the enemy.   He was on the point of gaining a complete victory, when Afendallos took to flight, accompanied by the Cretans, who were carried away in panic by his example.   Baleste, who in vain endeavoured to rally his forces, was surrounded and killed.

After his death all went badly for the Cretans; he was succeeded by a Spartan, who did not prove a success as a commander.   Retimo was revictualled by the Egyptian fleet, and the place was relieved.   With the troops thus set at liberty, the Egyptian commander, Ismail,* marched against the Greek army which was besieging Candia, and forced it to retreat with heavy loss.   For some unknown reason, Ismail was recalled in the height of his success, whereupon the Turks abandoned the offensive, which was resumed by the Greeks. Mano, the commander of the Greek army which had been besieging Candia, descended into the plains, and recommenced the siege of Retimo.   Candia was blockaded, the intention of the Cretans being to starve it out. Early in October the Christians were practically masters of the island.   Candia, Retimo, and Canea were blockaded both by land and sea, and it is confidently asserted that if the Greek authorities had despatched a force of

---

* Surnamed "Gibraltar," because he was the first Turk who sailed beyond the Straits of Gibraltar.

artillery and engineers, the whole island might have been won over to the Greek cause. But the incapable Afendallos was still in command, and there were reasons to believe that he had been bribed by the Turks. For the third time the Greeks demanded that he should be replaced by another commander ; the authorities sent out Tombazes, a chieftain of the island of Hydra, to take his place with the title of Harmost.

His arrival mended matters for a time ; he cleared the open country of the Turks, and laid siege to Canea. In February, 1823, the place would have capitulated, had it not been for the appearance of a Turkish fleet, which caused the siege of Canea to be abandoned. In the mean time, an Egyptian squadron on its way to Constantinople had touched at Casos, a small island about forty miles north-east of Crete, massacred the inhabitants, and then directed its course towards the latter. Unobserved by the Christians, the fleet entered the roadstead of Candia, and disembarked six thousand men, who were joined by the garrisons of Retimo and Canea. They marched into the interior, surprised a large number of villages, and massacred Christian men, women, and children, to the number of nearly twenty thousand. Eight hundred Sphakiotes, who had sought refuge in a large cave, were suffocated by the Turks, who piled up a heap of combustible matter before the entrance. Tombazes, despairing of rallying the dis-couraged Sphakiotes, fell on a small Turkish detachment with the Peloponnesian reinforcements and cut them to pieces. Encouraged by this success, the inhabitants came down again from the mountains, attacked the Turks as they were retiring to Retimo, and killed seven thousand of them. Tombazes applied for reinforcements, and three thousand men were sent to him, with whose aid he resumed the siege of Canea and Retimo.

On his part, the Sultan's powerful vassal, Mohammed Ali, Pasha of Egypt, made vigorous preparations for an attack upon Crete. The Turks in the island were reinforced by a fresh Egyptian expedition of ten thousand men, with a large squadron, under the command of Ismail Gibraltar. Ismail ravaged the island of Casos for the second time, and then disembarked his forces at Retimo. He incorporated with the reinforcements the troops which had been guarding Canea and Retimo, renewed the garrisons of these places, and, at the head of about twelve thousand men, advanced against the Sphakiotes. The latter fled to the mountains, and were followed by Ismail, who endeavoured to induce them to submit. His efforts were on the point of being completely successful, in spite of the opposition of a small minority of the Sphakiotes and Tombazes, when the news arrived that Sakhtoures had destroyed the Egyptian fleet, and had disembarked on the island; at the same time, a disturbance had broken out amongst the forces under Ismail's command. This caused negotiations between Ismail and the Sphakiotes to be broken off; hostilities were renewed, and lasted for eight days. The Greeks proved victorious; Ismail's army managed with great difficulty to make good its escape to Retimo, which was blockaded by Sakhtoures, and Sphakia was delivered from the invader. After another victory over a fresh Turkish fleet off Cape Spada, Sakhtoures was recalled. His recall proved disastrous to Crete; Ismail resumed the offensive, and Tombazes in vain asked for reinforcements from home. His own forces were too weak to continue the struggle, and, after making a final desperate effort which proved unsuccessful, he abandoned the island and returned to Hydra. He subsequently died at Anaphi (or Nanfi), one of the Cyclades, in September, 1824. A number of Cretans also left the island and repaired to Greece, where they fought bravely in the common cause.

The island submitted almost entirely, and became the arsenal of the Egyptians, who assembled there the troops with which they intended to attack the Morea. After the battle of Navarino (1827) a fresh insurrection broke out. An expedition set out from Nanphi under the command of Manuel Antoniades and Demetrius Calerges, and gained possession of Grabusa and Kissamos. In the mean time, the Christian inhabitants of the island retired to the mountains, watching for an opportunity to resume hostilities. Their hopes of annexation to Greece were overthrown by the action of the European Powers, who decided that Crete should not be included amongst the islands annexed to the newly formed state of Greece;* like Samos, it was restored to Turkish rule. Mohammed Ali, Pasha of Egypt, who had probably entertained ambitious designs of his own in regard to the island from the very first, continued to take a great part in its affairs, and in 1832 the Powers decided that it should be united to his government.

For a time things went well, Mohammed Ali being desirous of conciliating the Christians ; but at length the ruling passion of Turkish governors and officials—that

* Greece was declared independent February 3, 1830.

of extracting as much money out of their subjects as possible—gained the upper hand, and imposts were laid in quick succession upon the suffering islanders, who appealed to the Powers for the fulfilment of various promises which had chiefly been instrumental in inducing them to submit. The only result of this appeal was that orders were sent from Egypt to the governor of the island to put a considerable number of persons to death, apparently indiscriminately. From this time (1833) until 1840 the island was quiet.* In 1841 and 1858 other risings took place. During the latter year a petition was drawn up to the Sultan, asking relief from the most oppressive taxes, and, on a promise being given, the inhabitants abandoned the idea of insurrection. The promises made in 1850 by Abd-ul Medjid were repudiated by his successor, Abd-ul Aziz. In 1864 another assembly of the inhabitants was held, and another petition given to the governor, to be sent on to Constantinople. This governor, named Ismail, got up a counter-petition amongst his supporters on the island, in which it was declared the Cretans were perfectly satisfied with their lot. " The ensuing winter was one of great distress, and the spring passed without renewal of the disturbances or petitions; but in the autumn of that year, after my arrival in the island, I heard that there would be an assembly in the following spring, 1866. The discontent was very great. New taxes on straw, on the sale of wine, on all beasts of burden, oppressive collection of the tithes, together with short crops for two years in succession, had produced very great distress, and

---

* In 1840 the island was again handed over to the Sultan, in conse-quence of the rebellion of Mohammed Ali.

the governor added to these grievances his own extortions, with the most shameful venality in the distribution of justice, and disregard of such laws of procedure and punishment as existed. The councils were absolute mockeries, and the councillors his most servile tools."*

In May, 1866, certain influential Cretans, heads of villages, met together in the environs of Canea, and the same thing took place near Candia. But at present there was no idea of separation from Turkey, or desire for annexation to Greece. The governor wrote to Constantinople that the agitation was entirely due to the intrigues of Foreign Powers, especially Russia, and at the same time endeavoured to arouse the fanaticism of the Mussulman inhabitants of the island, by declaring that it was against them that the designs of the Christians were directed, and advising them to seek safety in their strongholds.

The Cretans refused to break up their assembly before they had received the Sultan's answer, and protested loudly that they entertained no evil designs against the Mussulmans. But Ismail had succeeded in hoodwinking the authorities at Constantinople; and the Sultan, instead of directing an inquiry into the grievances of the islanders, despatched eight thousand troops to Crete. The result of this was to irritate the Christians still further, and the assembly, increased by the representatives of all the villages, held a meeting at Omalos, a valley surrounded by mountains, at a little distance from Canea.

On the 26th of May, 1866, the assembly drew up the following list of the grievances which it demanded should be redressed : The taxes, instead of having been lessened since 1858, as had been promised, had been

* W. J. Stillman, *The Cretan Insurrection of* 1866-68.

increased. The dishonesty of the tithe-farmers. Taxes had been imposed upon salt, tobacco, wine, fish, butchers' meat, the sale of cattle, etc., and were collected with great harshness. The great lack of communication between different parts of the island, which had hindered the transport of the products of the interior. The various councils, which were supposed to be representative of the population, were really formed without the wishes of the latter being in any way consulted. The hard bargains made by the oil-merchants with the owners of olive trees. The arbitrary administration of justice. Although Greek was the universal language of the Cretans, both Mussulmans and Christians, all public documents were written in Turkish, and justice administered in that language. The evidence of Christians was practically invalid. The entire absence of schools in the agricultural districts. The reduction of the number of ports open for commerce to three. Religious intolerance. Lastly, the signatories declared that they had no idea of rebellion, and that they trusted to the Sultan to redress their grievances.

The Porte, after its usual dilatory fashion, sent no reply to this petition until the 23rd of July. It contained a refusal, and at the same time reinforcements were sent to the island, and Ismail Pasha was directed to use force, if necessary, in order to disperse the assembly. Meanwhile the Christians prepared to resist, and mustered, ten thousand strong, at Apocorona, to oppose the Turkish force, which now consisted of double that number. When hostilities had actually taken place, the assembly appealed (August 28) to the Consular representatives of the Powers, expressing their desire to be united to the mother-country, and on the 2nd of September declared the Turkish government abolished, and the island united to Greece. The Turkish arms had, in the mean time, suffered two reverses—at Apocorona and Selino. A message was sent from Constantinople, ordering all the inhabitants to lay down their arms. The firm front exhibited by the insurgents caused the Porte to recall Ismail, and replace him by the old governor, Mustapha Pasha Kiritli (the Cretan), as commissioner-extra-ordinary for the re-establishment of order. He also brought reinforcements with him, and soon had no less than forty thousand men at his disposal. The news of the outbreak of hostilities caused great excitement, not only at Athens, but throughout the East. Volunteers set out to join the insurgents, and committees were formed at Athens, with the object of supplying them with arms and provisions. On the 24th of October Mustapha utterly defeated the insurgents at Vafé, but hesitated to follow up his victory. The arrival of Coroneos, the ablest of the Greek chiefs, gave a fresh impetus to the insurrec-tion, after the first feelings of despondency had worn off. "Seeing the danger the insurrection was in, and the dissidence of its chiefs, he moved at once into the central provinces, and, collecting together such Cretans as he could find, surprised and cut off two small Turkish detachments, reawakened the enthusiasm of the islanders, gained for himself the prestige of victory, and rapidly recruited a considerable force." He established his headquarters at Arcadion, "whence he harassed the detachments which issued from Retimo, and kept alive the movement in the district between Sphakia and Mount Ida." In November Mustapha Pasha attacked the Monastery of Arcadion, in the east of the island. After an heroic resistance, the inmates were forced to capitulate ; it is said that the *Hegoumenos*, or Abbot, made an attempt to blow up the monastery, but the explosion only caused a breach in the walls, through which the Turks poured in, and massacred men, women, and children.

This incident aroused great enthusiasm, and increased the sympathy felt for the Cretans in Europe—especially in France, England, and Russia ; the insurgents were at the same time encouraged to persevere by the attitude adopted towards them by the diplomatists, who led them to hope for the intervention of the Powers in their favour. It seemed to be generally admitted that there was only one permanent solution of the question—the incorporation of Crete with the recently established kingdom of Greece ; although, at the present crisis, it seems difficult to arrive at a definite conclusion as to how far the inhabitants of Crete are themselves anxious to form part of the mother-country. In any case, in 1866 it was suggested that Crete should be made an independent state, under the suzerainty of the Porte, like the Danubian principalities.

In January, 1867, Lord Stanley, the English Foreign Minister, who had previously expressed suspicion of the motives of Russia, issued a despatch, in which he pointed out that the great difficulty in regard was the problem of the intermixture of races and creeds. Its case was different from that of Samos, which had an exclusively Christian population. He suggested that a Christian governor should be appointed, who was to be assisted by a council, in which Christians and

Mohammedans should have an equal number of votes; but the suggestion proved fruitless.

Disgusted at Mustapha Pasha's failure to put down the insurrection, the Turkish Government sent Server Effendi to Crete, and commissioned him to invite both religious parties to send deputies to Constantinople, and to offer the island a constitution similar to that of the Lebanon. The Sphakiote Christians scornfully rejected the proposal, and declared that any of the popular representatives who went to Constantinople would be looked upon as traitors to the cause of their co-religionists. At the same time, they set up a government of seven members in the name of King George of Greece; and Zimbrakakes, a Greek officer and Cretan by birth, who had been educated at the French school at Metz, issued a manifesto, in which he declared that the union of Crete to Greece was a matter that concerned the whole world. A suggestion that the question should be submitted to a plebiscite of the Cretans was declared to be impossible, in a remarkably vigorous circular addressed to the Powers by Fuad Pasha, the Turkish Foreign Minister, in which he declared that, if the Powers decided upon the annexation of Crete to Greece, another Navarino would be necessary. Finding attempts at negotiation useless, the Turkish Government decided to entrust Omar Pasha, its commander-in-chief and most experienced general, with the suppression of the insurrection. Russia and France again intervened, and endeavoured to prevent Omar Pasha beginning hostilities, and also again brought forward the question of a plebiscite; but the Sultan, who at first seemed inclined to assent to the proposal, afterwards refused, and there was nothing left for it but the continuance of hostilities. Omar Pasha was not very successful in his operations. His plan of campaign was to drive the insurgents back into the mountains of Sphakia, surround them, and cut them to pieces; but his attempt failed. What materially contributed to the prolongation of hostilities was the introduction of supplies and war materials from Greece. In spite of the efforts of Hobart Pasha, an Englishman who commanded the Turkish Navy, the Greek steamer managed to run the blockade successfully more than twenty times. At last, its captain, rather than allow it to fall into the hands of the Turks, set fire to it. It was replaced by another vessel which was called Enosis (*Union*).

On the 27th of August, 1867, the ambassadors of Russia, France, Prussia, and Italy, in Constantinople proposed a three months' cessation of hostilities, and the meeting of an international commission, to inquire into all the circumstances. The Porte agreed to a month's (not three months') cessation of hostilities, during which the blockade of Crete was to be continued, declared that it was impossible for it to discuss the question of its incorporation with Greece, although it was ready to listen to any other requests of the islanders, and promised to grant extensive reforms. On the 13th of September, an amnesty was proclaimed to those Cretans who were willing to lay down their arms and return to their homes; any of the inhabitants were to be at liberty to leave the island, provided they sold their property, and did not return without special permission from the Turkish Government. But the Cretans still hankered after the plebiscite, in view of the fact of the impending special investigation by the Powers. At last, Ali Pasha, the grand vizier, decided to go to Crete in person, with a brand new constitution in his pocket, which contained even more concessions than had been demanded; he met with anything but an enthusiastic reception, and his advances were repulsed, probably through the intrigues of Russia.

On the expiration of the armistice, Ali Pasha promulgated his programme of reforms, which contained the following provisions: * There was to be a Governor-General at the head of the civil administrative government, and a general at the head of the military garrison. The Governor-General was to be assisted by a council, formed of Mussulmans and Christians. Subordinate to the Governor-General were to be the governors of the *sandjak*, who were to be half Christian and half Mohammedan, while they were to have assistants of different religion to themselves. The districts were to be administered by sub-governors, and all these officials were to be nominated by the Government. Every governor was to be assisted by an administrative council, in that of the Governor-General, his two advisers, the president of the legal tribunals, the Greek metropolitan, the treasurer, and three Christian and three Mussulman representatives, chosen by their respective communities, were to have a seat and vote. No fresh tax was to be imposed without the sanction of

---

* The preamble is instructive in the light of subsequent events. " The losses and sufferings experienced by Crete, and which have been the sad result of disorders occurring in the island, have filled my heart with sorrow. Wishing before all things to remedy these evils, to secure to all the inhabitants indiscriminate happiness and prosperity," etc.

the general assembly; and all taxes to be remitted for two years. An annual Government grant to be made to the orthodox schools. Official correspondence was to be carried on in Greek and Turkish. All commercial, civil, and criminal cases between Christians and Mussulmans were to be decided by a mixed tribunal. A General Assembly was to be held yearly, to which every canton was to send two representatives. Crete was divided into twenty-two communes, each returning four deputies, two Christian and two Mohammedan; Sphakia returned four Christians. Every deputy was to be of Cretan birth, and a Turkish subject. The Assembly to meet in the Governor's house at Canea, and the session to be limited to forty days. These reforms were called the "Organic Statute," which, enlarged and modified eleven years later by the Convention of Halepa, is still supposed to be the constitutional charter of Crete.

On the 22nd of November, Ali Pasha opened the sitting of the Assembly of Deputies, in which there were only twenty-five Christians out of seventy-five members.

Omar Pasha, disgusted with his ill success and the incapacity of his generals, had retired from the command of the troops in the same month, and had been replaced by Hussein Avni Pasha; and towards the end of the year hostilities recommenced. The situation remained practically unaltered throughout the year 1868, neither Turks nor Cretans being able to gain any decisive advantage. On the 11th of December, an insult offered to the Turkish Ambassador gave the Porte an opportunity of delivering an ultimatum to Greece, demanding the disbanding of the volunteers, the disarming of the piratical vessels, the punishment of attacks upon Turkish subjects, and the discontinuance of the sending of supplies and ammunition to Crete. In the event of refusal, the Porte threatened to blockade the ports of Greece, bombard her commercial cities, and expel her merchants from the Turkish Empire ; at the same time, Omar Pasha was appointed commander-in-chief of the forces destined to operate against Greece. The Greek Government refused to accede to the terms of the ultimatum, the Turkish Ambassador left Athens, Greek subjects were ordered to leave Turkey, and war seemed inevitable. But, in view of the serious possibilities of the situation, the Powers (chiefly at the instance of Germany) proposed that a conference should be held in London and Paris ; the Porte accepted the proposal, on condition that its own ultimatum to Greece should form the basis of discussion. Towards the end of the year, the insurrection in Crete had come to an end, Petropoulakes, the Greek colonel, having surrendered. The conference, which was held in Paris early in 1869,* concluded its deliberations with a warning to Greece, that she should observe the same rules of conduct in dealing with Turkey as with the other Powers. It declared that Turkey had a just cause of complaint against Greece, but expressed the hope that the danger of war was over ; it was decided that Crete should continue a portion of the Turkish Empire, and not be annexed to Greece.

By an Imperial irade, a kind of constitution was bestowed upon the island, and a fixed system of taxation introduced. At the same time, in accordance with the stipulations of the Conference, a general amnesty was to

* February 18th.

G

be granted to all Cretan Christians. The Porte expressed its willingness to agree to this, but added a clause to its proclamation, to the effect that those who had not submitted and laid down their arms immediately after the promulgation of the "Organic Statute or Law" of 1868, as the constitutional charter of Crete was called, should be deprived of the benefit of it. As none of the insurgents had laid down their arms at the time, they found themselves excluded from the amnesty. The result was confiscation, imprisonment, fines, and insults of various kinds directed against the Christians. During the next four years, nothing of importance took place in the island.

In 1873, the Porte decreed a land-tax. The Cretans protested energetically, and threatened to take up arms. As the insurrection in Herzegovina had broken out about this time, the decree was revoked. From this time, periodical disturbances occurred in the island, the Porte attempting to evade the bestowal of the privileges which had been granted, and the islanders as vigorously claiming their rights. The Russo-Turkish War was the signal for a general rising, which was not suppressed without considerable difficulty.

In 1876, certain demands for administrative reform were submitted to the Porte, but the latter refused to grant them. The demands were as follows : That the Governor-General should be a Christian ; that public offices should be held by Christians in proportion to the total number of inhabitants ; that all public officials, whether Christian or Mohammedan, should be exclusively Cretan ; that all public documents should be published in Greek as well as in Turkish ; that the police should contain a preponderance of Christians in proportion to the population ; that the system of the administration of justice should be improved by the appointment of a supervising arbiter ; that a system of independent, municipal organization tending to decentralization should be established ; that the General Assembly should have the right to control the Agricultural Bank, and the erection of public buildings out of its profits ; that no taxes should be imposed in addition to those mentioned in the Organic Statute ; that reforms should be introduced in the system of public instruction ; that the seaports should be repaired, and means of inland communication increased ; the debt question to be settled ; the decree of exile against apostates to be cancelled, and liberty to be granted to restore and build places of Christian worship.

The debt question requires explanation. The Cretan farmers sell their olive oil to dealers at the seaports, who dispose of it at a large profit to the local exporters. The olive growers were careless about counting the amount they received in payment, being content to trust to the honesty of the dealers. These small proprietors, when in want of money, borrowed it from the dealers, at the same time pledging themselves to supply no one else. The tithe farmers also found themselves in arrears with the sum of money which they had contracted to supply to the Government ; they were compelled to offer it in small instalments, and, in order to provide these, had to apply to the dealers. Also, institutions called the " Orphans' Banks " were in the habit of advancing funds to the Cretan farmers at fifteen per cent., later, twelve per cent. interest. To the original sum must be added compound interest. In May, 1866, the private debts of the Cretans were said to have reached a total of 150,000,000 piastres, more than two-thirds of which were owing to Mussulman creditors. Some of the debtors abandoned their whole property to their creditors ; but in most cases the Government took possession of the property and sold it by public auction, reserving a dwelling and small piece of land for the owner. Hence, property became greatly depreciated in value, owing to the glut in the market, and frequently the amount realized by the sale was not enough to cover the amount of the debt.

As stated, the Porte refused to grant these demands, and it was with great difficulty that an insurrection was avoided. In 1877, the delegates of the Assembly renewed their petitions, and on receiving an unsatisfactory answer, withdrew to the mountains, and declared that they would not return to the towns until their demands were granted ; they remained in the mountains for more than a year, and forced all the Christians and some of the poorer Mohammedans to join them ; to add to the confusion, the law courts were closed. About Christmas, 1877, Hadji Mikhali landed in the island, and proceeded to levy taxes, enrol a police force, and administer justice. A few days later, Costaki Pasha arrived with the object of conciliating the insurgents, but they refused to treat with him except on their own terms.

At the end of January, 1878, the Assembly demanded that Crete should be made into a principality, and requested an answer within a week. No answer being received, the Committee broke off all negotiations on February 15th, and referred the case to the Powers, at the same time informing the Consuls that they had no intention of provoking hostilities. About a fortnight later, desultory hostilities having in the mean time broken out, a truce was arranged, and on March 26th the Assembly announced the election of a Provisional Government for the maintenance of order. The Turks, however, broke the truce, and the fighting continued.

By Article XXIII. of the Treaty of Berlin, "the Sublime Porte undertook scrupulously to apply in the Island of Crete the Organic Law of 1868, with such modifications as may be considered equitable." The Cretans were greatly disappointed that nothing more was done for them, and they solicited the intervention of England, at the same time declaring that the Organic Law was inadequate, and petitioning for a new form of government : either that their island should be placed under English protection, or, if that were impossible, be made a principality on the model of Samos.

On the 1st of September, Ahmed Mukhtar Pasha arrived as High Commissioner, and, after numerous conferences, a settlement, called the Pact or Convention of Halepa, was arrived at (October 25, 1878). Its articles were as follows :—*

ᵗ I. The Special Statute of the island of Crete is in force as heretofore ; certain provisions only of this statute shall be modified and completed as hereinafter stated. The Constitution shall not annul this statute.

II. The Governor-General is named in accordance with the Organic Statute of the island of Crete. The duration of his functions shall be for five years.

---

* See Hertslet, *Map of Europe by Treaty*, vol. iv. p. 2810.

III. The General Assembly shall be composed of eighty members, of whom forty-nine shall be Christians and thirty-one Mussulmans.

IV. The annual session of the General Assembly shall last forty days as heretofore. Nevertheless, if the Assembly cannot terminate the labours of this year within that time, the first session may be prolonged for twenty days in addition. The sittings shall be public.*

In order to supplement the deficiencies which exist in the Ottoman legislation now in force, the General Assembly shall have the right immediately to draw up a Code of Civil and Criminal Procedure, and a Communal Statute formulated by the Assembly, which shall be sanctioned by the Porte, provided they do not interfere with the rights of the Imperial Government, and if they are not contrary to the principles which govern the Ottoman laws and regulations.

If it be subsequently necessary to make modifications of a nature to supply deficiencies in regulations which are now in force, and which are demanded by requirements of purely local interests, the General Assembly shall have the right to submit, for the approval of the Sublime Porte, the modifications decided upon by a majority of two-thirds.

V. The number of the Christian Caïmakams † shall exceed that of the Mussulman Caïmakams, according to the requirements of the localities.

VI. The formation of the Administrative Councils shall take place as heretofore. Nevertheless, for the

---

* Previous to 1879 debates were held with closed doors.

† Sub-governors.

future, no Government official shall be a member of them, with the exception of the Vali, or Governor-General, the Governors, and Caïmakams, who will preside as a matter of right.

VII. The judicial power shall be distinct and separate from the Executive ; the composition of the Tribunals shall be the same as heretofore. Nevertheless, the Assembly may submit, for the approval of the Sublime Porte, a project of reorganization, which, while being more economical, will ensure a better administration of justice.

VIII. The Governor-General shall henceforth have an adviser, who shall be a Christian if he be a Mussulman, and *vice versa.*

IX. The general correspondence of the Vilayet, the *procès verbaux* of the Tribunals and Councils, shall be drawn up in two languages. But, as in general the Mussulman and Christian inhabitants of the island speak Greek, the deliberations of the General Assembly and the Tribunals shall take place in that language.

X. All the officials, with the exception of the Vali, shall be nominated subject to the laws and regulations in force. Natives, however, having the required qualifications, shall have the preference.

XI. Should the Assembly have to establish a new method of assessing the tithes, to protect more completely the interests of the Treasury and of the population at the same time, they must submit it to the sanction of the Government.

XII. Natives to be preferred in the formation of the gendarmerie, and recourse to be had to other inhabitants of the Empire in the event of an insufficiency of native candidates. The chief of the gendarmerie to be appointed by the Porte. The other officers to be chosen from both Christians and Mussulmans. A pension fund to be established for officers and soldiers, and a special regulation drawn up on the subject.

XIII. There shall be economy in the expenditure, The following items shall not be inserted in the budget of the island : The cost of the regular army ; the customs duties ; the taxes on salt and tobacco ; as also the receipts and expenditure on account of the "Vacouf" lands. which are now administered by the local authorities and shall henceforth be administered separately.

After the cost of local administration has been deducted from the revenue, the surplus shall be divided in equal parts between the Imperial Treasury and works of public utility, which shall be determined by the Assembly in the following order :—

1. Houses of detention.
2. Schools.
3. Hospitals.
4. Harbours and roads.

The Assembly shall have the right of examining whether the receipts and expenses have been applied according to the provisions of the budget for the year. In the event of these revenues not covering the expenditure, the Imperial Government will give to the administrative of the island a sum of money not exceeding the half of the import duties of the current financial year to meet the deficit in the salaries.

XIV. Paper money shall not be current in the island. The salaries of the officials shall be paid in specie.

XV. It shall be lawful for the inhabitants to found literary societies, printing presses, and newspapers, in conformity with the law of the Empire.

XVI. If Ministerial Ordinances are transmitted contrary to the independence of the tribunals, to the laws in force, and to the Organic Statute of the island, these ordinances shall not be put into execution.

Special provisions were also added, to the following effect : A general amnesty shall be proclaimed. The arrears of taxes shall not be exacted from the cultivators.

The inhabitants shall be permitted to keep their arms, but no one shall have the right to carry them without permission of the authorities. A definitive arrangement shall be adopted for debts contracted previous to 1866. Special offices shall be established in the island for agreement, and for all acts of sale of real property other than the acts of transfer, as well as for the registration of mortgages and deposits.

The firman was issued on the 28th of November, 1878, and the delay was taken as an indication of Turkish bad faith. On the 27th of November, a new governor, Caratheodori Pasha, arrived, but in less than three weeks was superseded by Photiades Pasha (14th of December).

He was a man of large sympathies, conciliatory, and proved himself a most capable official. The terms in which he addressed the Assembly are worth quoting, as showing his enlightened views. " One of your first duties," he said, " is the elaboration of a code of civil and criminal procedure and of a municipal law, the organization of the legal tribunals, the introduction of a better system of taxes, and the administration and regulation of the finances ; it will be your duty to deliberate concerning works of public usefulness, the regulation of the debts of the agricultural population, and other matters provided for by the ' Organic Law.' " After Photiades had governed the island for seven years, he resigned in 1885, owing to a dispute about the question of *vakoufs*, that is to say, tithes for the benefit of Mussulman religious establishments, which were exacted from certain Christian villages. He was succeeded by Savas Pasha, an orthodox Epirote Greek. The inhabitants at first refused to accept him as governor ; the Christian members of the Assembly issued several proclamations, decided to refuse to pay the taxes, declared all magistrates traitors who took orders from Savas, and provisionally intrusted the Christians with the maintenance of public order. The agitation did not subside until Savas, after the consular representatives had intervened, solemnly promised, in the presence of the Cretan parliament assembled in the Episcopal church, to govern in accordance with the laws, and further, to resign his office, in case any serious dispute should arise between him and the majority of the representatives. In September, 1885, the Roumelian revolt took place, and the Cretans determined to demand union with Greece, if the union of Bulgaria and Roumelia was maintained. On the 21st of December, the Cretans addressed to the representatives of the Powers at Constantinople a memorandum, in which they asserted that the Powers had on several occasions recognized their right to union with the mother-country ; that the circumstances seemed favourable for carrying it out ; and that the local institutions were insufficient and lacked the necessary authority. Two requests, formulated by the Assembly, were unfavourably received at Constantinople. According to the existing arrangement, laws proposed to the Assembly were passed by a majority of votes, but did not become law until the sanction of the Sultan had been obtained ; and when it was a question of amending laws already in existence, two-thirds of the votes were necessary. The deputies demanded that a simple majority should be sufficient in the case of amendments, and that the approval of the Sultan should not be delayed longer than three months. They also demanded certain changes in the financial administration of the island, especially in regard to custom-house duties.

We do not hear much of the island until 1889, when an outbreak took place, which had its origin in quarrels amongst the Christian population, who subsequently united against the Turks. The insurgents demanded the appointment of a new governor, and the reform of the constitution. A new governor was ordered by the Porte to establish a state of siege in the island, to institute courts-martial, and to call upon the rebels to lay down their arms. Towards the end of the year the disturbances quieted down, and the Porte proclaimed a general amnesty ; but this amnesty was found to be deceptive, since all who had been imprisoned were excluded from participation in it, and all the Christian judges of the Court of Appeal resigned as a protest. The Sultan was afterwards induced to alter it, and all the inhabitants, with few exceptions, were allowed to be included in it. Later on we have the usual tale of outrages and massacres. In 1891 the mayors of several eparchies informed the British Consul at Canea that the Turkish Government was entirely unable to maintain order, and that the Christians would be obliged to take up arms in self-defence. There was some fighting between the Turkish troops and a band of insurgents. In 1892 disturbances arose in consequence of infractions of the Organic Statute; meetings were held, and dispersed with violence. Owing to the intervention of the Bishop of Sphakia, hostilities stopped; but the seizing of several Cretans on a charge of conspiracy by the Government caused a renewal of the rising. Matters went on in much the same way until 1894, when the execution of four Christians led to serious disturbances, chiefly because certain Mussulmans, who had also been sentenced to death, had been pardoned, with the exception of one. The Assembly of Representatives from all parts of the island met at Canea, and addressed a petition to the Sultan, begging him to alter the system of taxation, to convoke the General Assembly, and to nominate a Christian governor whose appointment should be a permanent one. The Turkish governor was shot at, and on the same day superseded.

Early in 1895, in answer to the petition addressed to him, the Sultan issued a firman, ordering elections for the General Assembly to take place. The number of deputies was reduced from eighty to fifty-seven, and included thirty-five Christians and twenty-two Mussulmans; in the same year another petition was drawn up, demanding the restoration of the "Organic Statute" * and

---

* The Pact of Halepa had practically been abrogated by an Imperial Firman of November, 1889.

the reorganization of the system of taxation and police. Measures were immediately taken to break up, by force of arms, the meeting which had drawn up this petition. This and the seizure of a number of Christian notables led to a rising, a reform committee was formed, and an engagement took place between the Turkish troops and the insurgents, followed by acts of plunder and pillage, which were unchecked by the Turkish authorities. At length, the ambassadors at Constantinople induced the Porte to publish an edict, convoking the National Assembly at Canea ; Georgios Berovitch Pasha, a Christian, was appointed Governor-General with Hassan Pasha as vice-governor. A proclamation declaring a general amnesty was issued (July 2), and the Constitution or Pact of Halepa was restored. The National Assembly was opened on the 13th, and petitions and counter-petitions were drawn up by the Christians and Mussulmans. As the island still continued in a highly disturbed condition, it was suggested that it should be blockaded, so as to prevent assistance being sent to it from Greece ; but the project was dropped, owing to the refusal of England to co-operate. The Reform Committee, which had been formed in the early part of the year, gave place to a Revolutionary Assembly, which was headed by one of the prominent leaders of the 1868 revolution. Later on, the Sultan expressed his willingness to carry out any reforms which the ambassadors of the great Powers might demand. The following proposals were put before him as indispensable : The appointment of a Christian governor for five years, subject to the approval of the Powers ; the reorganization of the police system ; the island to be autonomous, except that it was to pay an annual tribute to Turkey ; and both civil and military powers to be united in the hands of the governor ; it was also suggested that two-thirds of the public appointments should be given to the Christians, and one-third to the Mussulmans. The Sultan approved the scheme, which was also accepted by the deputies, and it seemed as if at last a definite settlement had been found. Georgios Berovitch was appointed as the first Christian Governor-General on the 11th of September. The hopes of the diplomatists were, however, doomed to be disappointed. The usual delay on the part of the Turks in carrying out the promised reforms, the want of a regularly organized police force, and the non-administration of justice, caused a feeling of discontent amongst the people, and fresh disturbances took place.

The intervention of Greece and the events of the last six months are too familiar to need description ; at present it is impossible to foresee the result of events upon the island. The Powers have offered almost complete independence to the insurgents, who, as far as can be ascertained, refuse to accept it, and declare that they will be satisfied with nothing less than annexation to Greece, which the great Powers are unwilling to permit. In spite of the landing of Greek forces in Crete, hostilities have not as yet broken out between Turkey and Greece,* although, at the moment of writing, it is reported that a band of Greek insurgents has crossed the Turkish frontier, and that severe fighting has taken place. Who knows whether this may not be the spark destined to set the powder-magazine of Europe ablaze, and to bring

* Written April 12th.

about the very catastrophe which the intervention of the Powers has striven to avert.

The following statements in regard to Crete, although from an avowedly pro-Hellenic source, may be accepted in the main : (*a*) "That the Cretans have at all times shown an unalterable determination to shake off foreign rule, of whatever form." (*b*) "That their irrevocable wish to be united to the mother country has been manifested and proclaimed on each successive rising." (*c*) "That the one constant and invariable result of the intervention of the Powers in the affairs of Crete has been the re-imposition of the yoke of Turkey on the unfortunate islanders." (*d*) "That the Powers have never succeeded in insuring to the Cretans the fulfilment of the reforms which they promised to exact from Turkey; and that the three measures of autonomy under Turkish rule— the Organic Law of 1868, the Halepa Pact of 1878, and the Convention of 1896—have proved illusory."

CHAPTER V.

GREEK HETÆRIÆ AND THE WAR OF INDEPENDENCE.

THE events of the last few days* have drawn attention to the association known as the *Ethnikē Hetæria,* which is understood to be one of the powerful factors in the present movement, and was also undoubtedly the direct organizer of the advance into Turkish territory, all responsibility for which is disavowed by the Greek Government. For the moment the centre of interest has shifted from the Mediterranean to the frontiers of Macedonia, where the regular armies of Greece and Turkey, with their patience by this time almost exhausted, stand facing each other, waiting for orders. Under these circumstances, it will be interesting to enter into some little detail as to the parent societies of the powerful "Union," the name of which stands at the head of this chapter, and which is said to possess greater authority and influence over the Greek people than even the King himself. Even in ancient times such associations flourished in Greece, and were formed (especially at Athens) with the object of assisting the oligarchic against the democratic party. In 411 B.C., it was mainly owing to them that an attempt was made to abolish the democratic constitution, and their

* Written April 14th.

influence materially contributed to the triumph of Sparta over Athens in the Peloponnesian War. In the times of the Byzantine Empire, the word *Hetæria* was used to denote certain "regiments" or "companies" of the imperial guard, composed exclusively of foreigners ; their special duty was to guard the Emperor's person, and attend him on the occasion of important ceremonials.

During modern times, the national aspirations of the Greeks, encouraged by the events of the French Revolutionary period, and the downfall of the Turkish power promised by Napoleon's expedition to Egypt, gave birth to a "political" *Hetæria*, founded by Constantinos Rhigas, the Tyrtæus of Modern Greece, at the end of the last century, a most accomplished man, and the author of several literary works. He was born at Velestino (the ancient *Pheræ*), in Thessaly, and was for some time in the service of the *Hospodar* * of Wallachia. The French Revolution inspired him with the idea of bringing about a general rising of the Greeks, with the object of shaking off the Turkish yoke. In pursuance of this idea, he travelled through Greece and formed a numerous association of patriots, who were recruited from all classes of society, and even included some Turkish pashas. His first adherents were the Greek *Klephts*, for whom he composed a number of warlike songs.† Everything was ready for the outbreak of a national movement, when the entry of the French into Italy highly excited the hopes of the Greeks. Rhigas resolved to apply directly to Bonaparte, with whom he

---

* A title formerly borne by the vassal princes of Moldavia and Wallachia.

† See a specimen in chap. vi.

carried on a correspondence for several months. After the French had reached Venice, he left Vienna, where he had been living for some time, with the intention of having a personal interview with Bonaparte. Shortly before his departure for Trieste, he sent on to one of his friends there a box containing some copies of his poems and his correspondence with Bonaparte. On his arrival at Trieste, he was arrested and taken to Vienna. After he had been imprisoned for some time, he was handed over to the Turkish Governor of Belgrade. Fruitless efforts were made to save his life, for he was beheaded, or, according to others, drowned in the Danube by the Pasha's order. His last words are said to have been : "I have sown the seed in the furrow ; the hour is approaching when my people will reap the harvest." The death of Rhigas for a while checked the movement which he had inaugurated.

We ought here to mention the name of Adamantinos′ Corass, a native of Chios (1748–1833), a distinguished literary man. His wide reading of ancient Greek literature inspired him with a love of freedom and hatred of Turkish rule. He decided to leave his native island and travel. In 1788 he went to Paris. The Revolution created a deep impression upon him, and he decided to remain in France and preach the doctrine of Greek independence. For this object he recognized that it was of great importance to bring home to the Greeks their glorious past, to purify their language, and make them act in a manner calculated to win for them the sympathy of Europe ; and to this task he devoted the remainder of his life. He died and was buried at Paris ; the following inscription, composed by himself, was written upon his tombstone: "Here lies Adamantinos Corass ; a foreign soil covers me, but I loved Paris as dearly as I loved Greece, my native land."

In 1812 was founded the *Hetæria Philomousos*, which may be translated "the literary," or "liberal education" society. Its object was to found schools throughout Greece, to collect funds for the preservation of ancient monuments and for carrying on fresh excavations, to establish a library and a museum at Athens, to publish editions of the Greek classics, and to assist young Greeks with sums of money, in order to enable them to complete their education at the universities. This association obtained a considerable success, and counted amongst its members a number of learned men from all parts of Europe, notably Count Capo d'Istria : it is said to have numbered eighty thousand members. It was a praise-worthy and perfectly harmless institution, but not likely to be of much practical use in assisting Greece to regain her freedom, if it had ever entertained any such idea. During the revolution of 1821 the *Hetæria* almost disappeared : it was re-established in 1824, but was rendered unnecessary by the formation of Greece into an independent kingdom.

Two years after the foundation of the "*Hetæria Philomousos*" another league was formed (1814), called the "*Philikē Hetæria*," or "friendly society." It was founded in Odessa by a Greek merchant, Scouphas, of Arta, and two young men, one of whom was a free-mason. The warning afforded by the fate of Rhigas caused the strictest secrecy to be observed. The society was national and political, and had for its object nothing less than the total overthrow of the Ottoman dominion with the assistance of Russia, and the setting-up of a Greek kingdom, with Constantinople as the capital : at the same time, the heads of it were clever enough to shelter themselves behind the "*Hetæria Philomousos,*" pretending that it was merely a branch of it. It was framed on the model of a freemasons' lodge ; even the initiated did not know who was at the head of it, but there were not wanting mysterious hints that it was no less a personage than the Czar of Russia himself, which gained for the society a considerable reputation. In 1818 it changed its *locale* to Constantinople, brought its organization to a high state of efficiency, and despatched emissaries throughout all the countries inhabited by Greeks : several influential personages, Prince Nicolas, Georgios and Demetrios Ypsilantes, Prince Alexander Mavrocordatos, and the Patriarch of Constantinople became members of it.

In a very short time the society had extended its influence far and wide, even to the savage tribes of the mountainous country in the neighbourhood of Sparta. It felt the necessity of having a publicly-recognized head of ability and distinction. The management fixed its choice upon one of two persons—Count Capo d'Istria, minister of the Russian Emperor, and the young prince Alexander Ypsilantes, son of a former *hospodar* of Wallachia, who had fought with distinction for Russia, and was at the time in high favour with the Czar. Capo d'Istria refused, but Ypsilantes accepted the position, believing that he would be acting in accordance with the wishes of Russia. This was on the 20th of June, 1820. He immediately sent out secret proclamations to all the general-ephors, or superintendents, asking for arms and money. The rising of Theodore Vladimiresko, one of the lesser *boyards*, or nobles, of Wallachia, against the oppression of the superior *boyards* and Fanariotes, was regarded by the Hetærists as the signal for a rising against Turkey. In the eighteenth century the Turks had introduced, in regard to its Wallachian vassals, the system of selling the office of *voivode*, or *hospodar*, to the highest bidder at Constantinople, to be farmed out. The princes were mostly Greeks from the Fanar quarter of Constantinople, hence the name Fanariotes, who had been dragomen, or held some court office. Before he had received any definite proof of the sympathetic co-operation of Russia, Ypsilantes found himself committed to the dangerous undertaking of raising the standard of revolt in Moldavia ; and he could not draw back since one of his messengers had been arrested in Servia, and the whole undertaking had been betrayed. Together with his brother and a small following, he crossed the Pruth, and, at Jassy, informed the Moldavians of the resolve of the Greeks to shake off the Turkish yoke, invited them to keep quiet, but summoned all the Greeks to follow the banner of freedom. According to his plan of operations, the Greeks throughout the whole of Turkey were to rise at the time of his advance into Moldavia. This general rising did not, however, take place, as the Porte had received previous information of the designs of the Hetærists, and had taken the utmost precautions to foil them. Russia, on whose direct assistance Ypsilantes had counted, and which he had already promised to the Greeks, expressed disapproval of his proceedings ;

he was excluded from the military service of Russia, all help definitely refused him, and the entire responsibility for anything that happened was laid upon himself. The troops in the Pruth and in Bessarabia were ordered to observe the strictest neutrality, and the Russian ambassador at the Porte expressed the Czar's disapproval of the revolutionary attempt. Ypsilantes and the Hetærists were thus thrown entirely upon their own resources. The Hospodar of Moldavia, Michael Soutzo, certainly declared in their favour, but the *Boyards* remained loyal to Turkey, and Vladimiresko at Bucharest looked upon them as no better than Fanariotes, against whose oppressions his rising in Wallachia had been mainly directed, and he therefore refused to have anything to do with them. However, Ypsilantes marched to Bucharest, whence he issued an appeal to the Wallachians, with the object of winning them over to the cause of freedom. But he failed in the attempt; the revolution in the Morea, which broke out during this time, and the terrible scenes which took place in Constantinople, where thousands of Greeks lost their lives in the attempt to secure for themselves an independent nationality, discouraged the Moldavians and Wallachians, who were, further, disgusted with the scandalous behaviour of certain persons in the Prince's suite and the want of discipline amongst his troops. A number of Ypsilantes' own adherents began to waver. Finding himself, therefore, obliged to act strictly on the defensive, Ypsilantes took up his position at Tergorisht, in the centre of Wallachia, where he threw up entrenchments, and declared that he would await the advance of the Turks, who had assembled in considerable forces, and met with no serious opposition in marching to

Jassy and Bucharest. Vladimiresko, who had succeeded in regaining possession of Bucharest, now threw off the mask, and entered into negotiations with Kara Mustapha, Pasha of Silistria, to whom he handed over the city. He was accused of treachery and put to death by Ypsilantes. After the Turkish victory at Dragashan, in which the Hetærist corps called the Sacred Band distinguished itself by the greatest bravery, the insurrection was at an end. Ypsilantes fled to Austria, where he was detained as a prisoner until 1827, when he was released, but died in the following year. " The flight of Ypsilantes was the last scene of the drama enacted by the Philikē Hetæria in the provinces, where the rash ambition of its supreme head and the utter incapacity of its members brought great calamity on the people, and laid the foundations of an anti-Greek feeling, which resulted [at that time] in depriving the Greeks of all political power in those provinces, but was not entirely without good effect, since it contributed to develop projects of national independence. It was reserved for the native land of the Hellenic race to prove that Greece could still arm heroes in her cause." * When the war of independence resulted in the establishment of the Kingdom of Greece, the Philikē Hetæria lost its influence as a political factor for a time.

But, although less demonstratively, it still continued its work—a work which cannot be said to be complete while so many thousands of Greek-speaking people, both on the mainland and in the islands, such as Crete and Samos, remain more or less directly subject to Turkish rule. The avowed object of the society was,

---

* Finlay, *History of Greece*, vol. vi. p. 134.

and is, to promote the knowledge of Greek literature, and to restore, as far as possible, the language of Ancient Greece in place of Romaic, which is a mixture of Greek, Turkish, and Italian. Its efforts have certainly been crowned with success as far as the written language of newspapers, etc., is concerned, although, in spite of assertions to the contrary, this pseudo-classical tongue is a broken reed for the ordinary traveller to depend upon. In addition to this, the society does its utmost, not unnaturally, to imbue the rising generation with a patriotic hatred of the Turks. The society, which now appears to be called Ethnikē (National), numbers amongst its members the most influential and wealthy of the Greeks. It is stated that the King and his ministers are members of it, and if so, it is easy to understand how difficult it is for him to hold them back ; in fact, we may say that, at the present moment, the ruling power in Greece is the Ethnikē Hetæria. The distinctive dress is a round cap without any peak, on the front of which is a small gold-embroidered device—a cross with the letters E.E. beneath, and a globe above. Special correspondents have recently given interesting accounts of the manner in which the bands organized by the society were sent on their mission across the frontier, accompanied by the solemn blessings pronounced by the priests. As the Greeks have probably by this time lost all confidence in the disinterestedness of Russia, the society will find new scope for its energies in endeavouring to prevent the realization of the designs of that power, designs which have as their goal Constantinople, the ancient capital of the Byzantine or Lower Empire, which it is the dream of the Greeks to revive, as their inheritance by right,

It is generally considered that the rebellion of Ali Pasha of Janina against the Turkish Government, and the intrigues of the Philikē Hetæria and Russian agencies, were the chief causes of the Greek Revolution. Mr. Finlay, who dissents from this view, has the following remarks upon this society : " The power of secret societies is very apt to be overrated, and in no case has the influence of a secret political society been more unduly magnified than in the case of the Philikē Hetæria. Many of the best Hetærists were more directly under the influence of Russian orthodoxy than of Hellenic independence, and many of the best men who distinguished themselves in the Greek Revolution were not Hetærists. The first members of the Philikē Hetæria were bankrupt merchants and intriguing adventurers, possessed of some cunning and great enthusiasm. Turkey was supposed to be on the eve of dissolution, and Russia to be on the point of gaining possession of Constantinople. The Hetæria was formed when these ideas were predominant, and it prospered. In all probability it would soon have expired of inanition had it not been kept alive by its members making use of the name of the Czar of Russia, who was generally supposed to grant it his secret protection. The influence of secret societies or national movements can only be powerful when these movements coincide with the general impulse to which the societies owe their own impulse. The schemes of the Hetærists of Odessa were wild and visionary—the object of the inhabitants of Greece was definite and patriotic. The Hetærists proposed to set fire to Constantinople, to burn the arsenal, to destroy the fleet, to assassinate the Sultan, and bring about a general massacre of the Mussulman population. They overlooked the possibility of millions of warlike Mohammedans rushing to Constantinople to defend the Turkish domination, who, when the conspirators had destroyed the fountain-head of all the vices of the Ottoman administration, might have laid the foundations of a new and more powerful Turkish Empire."

A brief outline of the chief events of the Greek War of Independence may suitably close this chapter.

The defeat of Ypsilantes and the " Sacred Band" put an end to the rising in the Danubian Principalities ; but the fire of revolution was kindled in Greece. In March, 1821, Germanos, Bishop of Patras, summoned his countrymen to arms and made himself master of Calavryta. The Arcadians rose under Colokotrones, the Mæniotes under Mavromikhales, and a National Assembly was formed at Kalamata, called the Senate of Messenia, to undertake the direction of the movement. Its rapid success roused the fury of the Turks, and great cruelties were committed by them in Constantinople and the cities of Asia. These cruelties caused public opinion to turn in favour of the Greeks ; the insurrection became general, and the first campaign was attended with brilliant results.

Encouraged by this, the Greeks decided to organize a central Government. In December, 1821, a National Assembly of sixty-seven deputies was convoked at Argos and transferred to Epidaurus. Its first proceeding was to declare the independence of Greece ; after which, it drew up a provisional constitution, called the " Organic Statute " of Epidaurus. As president of the new state, a Fanariote prince, Mavrocordatos, was appointed, with a Secretary of State to assist him. The new government signalized its liberality by a decree for the abolition of slavery; it also passed an edict for compensation for military services, and for a provision for the widows and orphans of those slain in battle; while a third edict regulated the internal administration of the provinces. A proclamation was issued to the effect that Greece was now an independent federal state, and a blockade of Turkish towns was declared. Europe, however, did not view the action of Greece with approval; France was neutral, England distinctly hostile, while Russia and Austria expressed an unfavourable opinion of the insurrection. The Sultan endeavoured to gain the favour of Russia, and made extensive preparations for war. Ali Pasha of Janina was killed; a considerable fleet was assembled at Constantinople, while Mohammed Ali, Pasha of Egypt, equipped another. In April, 1822, the Turks carried out a fearful massacre in Chios (Scio), butchering in cold blood twenty-three thousand of its inhabitants, and selling forty-seven thousand women and children as slaves. During this time the Greek fleet was very successful, under the command of Miaoules and Canares, whose fire-ships inflicted great damage upon the Turkish fleet. Mavrocordatos, who had been betrayed by an Albanian chief and utterly defeated at Peta, reorganized his army, and entrenched himself at Missolonghi, on the north side of the Gulf of Patras. Omar Vriones began the siege which ended with the total destruction of his army; he lost his artillery and baggage, was defeated on the Achelous, and returned to Prevesa with a decimated army. Unfortunately, dissensions broke out amongst the Greek leaders, who were divided into two factions ; the captains or military chiefs, like Mavromikhales and Colocotrones, and the political chiefs, like Mavrocordatos and Demetrios Ypsilantes ; and, in spite of insurgent successes, the insurrection did not become general, neither Macedonia, nor Thessaly, nor even Epirus, following the example of Greece.

The intervention of Egypt turned the balance in favour of Turkey. Mohammed Ali, Viceroy of Egypt, sent his fleet to the Archipelago ; Ibrahim Pasha, his son, landed in Peloponnesus with twenty thousand men, carried everything before him, and the Greeks lost nearly everything that they had acquired. Meanwhile, Reshid Pasha had laid siege to Missolonghi, the outpost of Hellenic independence. The siege lasted eleven months, from the 27th of April, 1825, to the 22nd of April, 1826 ; its heroic defence excited the impassioned sympathy of the whole of Europe, and volunteers of various nationalities flocked to its assistance. It is hardly necessary to mention the name of Lord Byron, who was unremitting in his exertions on behalf of the Greeks, except to state that he always seemed to be under the impression that the dissensions amongst the Greek leaders themselves would, in the end, render their undoubtedly heroic and in the main patriotic efforts futile. After a lengthened blockade, Missolonghi was at length taken by assault.

Their good fortune seemed to have deserted the Greeks in the following year. Athens was taken in May by the Turks, soon after the arrival of Lord Cochrane, who was appointed admiral of the Greek fleet. The resistance of the Greeks seemed broken, and at this moment the great Powers of Europe thought the time had come for them to intervene. The accession of the Czar Nicholas to the throne of Russia, and of Canning to power in England, were two facts in favour of Greece, and an arrangement (the Treaty of London) was concluded between England, Russia, and France (July 6, 1827) with the object of putting an end to the devastating war, and of establishing the independence of Greece, under certain tributary stipulations. This treaty was presented to the Porte on the 18th of August ; in the mean time the Greek Government proclaimed an armistice in conformity with the Treaty of London ; but the Turkish Government decided to reject the intervention of the three Powers. The Greeks thereupon resumed hostilities, and an accident, the "untoward event" of Navarino, materially assisted their cause. The fleets of England, Russia, and France were cruising about the coasts of Peloponnesus, to prevent the Turkish fleet ravaging the Greek islands. Winter coming on, the admirals thought it more prudent to anchor in the bay of Navarino (the ancient bay of Pylus), on the south-west coast of the Morea. The first shots were fired from the Turkish side, and two Englishmen were killed. This was the signal for hostilities. The Turkish fleet was practically annihilated ; not more than fifteen vessels escaped without damage, and more than five thousand Turks were killed. In this manner, an engagement which had begun in consequence of an accident, ended in the almost complete destruction of the naval power of Turkey, which she has never recovered. Enraged at the battle of Navarino, the Porte seized all the ships of the Christian Powers that were at Constantinople, and broke off all communication with the allied Powers, until an indemnity should have been paid for the destruction of the fleet ; at the same time the ambassadors left Constantinople ; the Porte, however, pretended to desire peace, while in reality it was making extensive preparations for war.

Shortly afterwards, early in 1828, Capo d'Istria, who had been in the service of Russia, was appointed President of the Greek Government. His first measures were to establish a high national council and national banks, and to put the military on a fresh footing. All attempts at mediation between Greece and the Porte seemed hopeless, since the latter rejected every proposal, In the mean time, France, acting in agreement with England, sent some troops to the Morea, and an arrangement was come to, by which Ibrahim Pasha undertook to withdraw his troops and to set at liberty a number of Greek prisoners whom he had sent as slaves to Egypt. To defend the Morea from the chance of fresh invasions by Turkey, the Powers drew up a declaration to the effect that they intended to place the Morea and the Cyclades Islands under their protection until a definite arrangement should have been arrived at in regard to the provinces of which they had taken possession, and that the entrance of any military force into the country would be looked upon as an attack on themselves ; they also requested the Porte to suggest a definite settlement in regard to Greece. Hostilities, in the mean time, continued, great excesses being committed by the Turks, who even went so far as to burn down the olive-groves.

The basis of a settlement was, however, at last

agreed upon between the Great Powers. By the Protocol of London, signed by Russia, France, and England on the 22nd of March, 1829, it was decided to limit the boundaries of Greece to a line drawn from the Gulf of Arta to the Gulf of Volo ; the Greeks were to pay an annual tribute of one million five hundred thousand piastres to the Sultan ; a joint commission, composed of Turks and Greeks, was to be appointed to determine the question of the indemnification of the Turks for the loss of property in Greece ; Greece was to enjoy a qualified independence, under the sovereignty of the Porte ; the government was to be in the hands of an hereditary Christian Prince, chosen by the Sultan ; at every succession of the hereditary prince, a year's tribute was to be paid, mutual amnesty was to be declared, and all Greeks were to be allowed a year to sell their property and leave Turkish territory.

But it was a long time before the state of things in Greece attained to anything like a settled condition. Capo d'Istria, the President, found himself in a position of great embarrassment. He had undoubtedly done his best for the maintenance of order, the suppression of brigandage and piracy, and the formation of a regular army ; the establishment of courts of justice and schools ; of means for collecting the revenue, and providing for the material wants of the population. His idea was to organize Greece on the model of a European state ; but his ideas of government were Russian, and, ruling with a high hand, he gave great offence to the masses of the people, who, jealous of all foreign influence, showed themselves determined to resist the imposts and sanitary measures of the new form of government. A fifth meeting of the National Assembly took place at Argos (July 23–August 18, 1829), at which the *Panhellenium*, or council of twenty-seven members, composed of the chief notabilities of Greece, was replaced by a Senate, which only had a consultative voice. At this meeting Capo d'Istria delivered a long address, in which he gave an account of the state of the country and the measures he had in view for the organization of the army and finances. It was agreed that troops should be raised in order to deliver the whole of Greece from Turkish rule, but there was no money; out of sixteen million piastres, the army estimates absorbed fifteen million, and even this sum was far from being adequate for its purpose. The terrible struggle which had been continued for six years had exhausted the resources of the country; nearly a quarter of the population had perished; the olive groves had been devastated, and the fields had remained untilled for several years.

After the issue of the Protocol of London, the Powers requested that the troops of the Provisional Government should be withdrawn from Northern Greece, and that the blockade of the fortresses occupied by the Turks outside the Morea and the Cyclades should be raised. The defeat of Turkey by Russia (who had declared war in April), which culminated in the humiliating Treaty of Adrianople (September 14, 1829), led to the drawing up of a fresh Protocol, relative to the independence of Greece, signed by the representatives of England, France, and Russia. By this it was decreed that Greece was to "form an independent State, and enjoy all the rights, political, administrative, and commercial, attached to complete independence; the Greek Government was to be monarchical and here-ditary, and confided to a Prince who shall not be capable of being chosen from among those of the families reigning in the states that signed the Treaty of the 6th July, 1827 [*i.e.* Great Britain, France, and Russia], and who shall bear the title of Sovereign Prince of Greece, the choice of that Prince to form the subject of subsequent communications and stipulations."* Eubœa and the Sporades Islands were left to Greece, and its frontier was fixed at a line drawn from the mouth of the river Achelous or Aspropotamos (White River) from Vrakhori to the Bay of Zeitun. The National Assembly refused to agree to these clauses. Prince Leopold of Saxe-Coburg, who was offered the crown of Greece, at first accepted it on the 20th of February, 1830, but subsequently refused it, on the plea that the Greeks themselves were unfavourably disposed towards him, and that they were dissatisfied with the arrange-ments that had been made as to the boundaries of the newly-constituted kingdom. The Greeks themselves were divided. Capo d'Istria, whose desire it was to organize them off-hand after a European fashion, took as his model the Russian bureaucracy, apparently under the idea that, after four centuries of oppression, they needed a strong hand to make them appreciate thoroughly the blessings of their recently-recovered freedom. The country landowners supported him, but the liberals formed a *syntagmatic,* or constitutional party. All opposition was put down by the President with

---

* For the above somewhat confused wording the language of diplomacy is responsible.

great severity, which only had the effect of irritating and increasing the opposition. A provisional government was set up at Hydra by Miaoules, Conduriotes, and Tombazes; Ipsara and Syra joined in. The imprisonment of Mavromikhales provoked an insurrection of the Mainotes of Peloponnesus, who demanded a constitution. Miaoules captured the Greek fleet in the harbour of Poros, and, finding himself blockaded by a Russian squadron, set fire to it. The rupture between the old leaders of the insurrection and the Government was complete; Miaoules, Mavrocordatos, and Conduriotes were declared traitors. On the 9th of October, 1831, at six o'clock in the morning, while on his way to church, Capo d'Istria was accosted by the brother and son of Mavromikhales. When he was in the act of taking off his hat to return their salute, one fired a pistol at him and the other stabbed him in the side; his wounds immediately proved fatal. One of his assassins was slain by the people, the other found refuge in France. It was unfortunate that the death of Capo d'Istria occurred when it did. In a few days the Congress would have assembled, and the decisions of the three Great Powers would have established a new order of things, which would have allowed the President to resign with honour an authority which had been impaired by obstacles and opposition of various kinds, but which he could not have handed over to his political opponents of his own free will, without the risk of increasing the confusion. When their passions had once calmed down, his fellow-citizens would have been forced to recognize in him the eminent qualities which had gained for him throughout Europe so many friends of distinction. One of these, M. Eynard, has thus described his character : "The President of Greece was founded upon an antique model; he was austere, strict, and a man of unrivalled honesty; he never sought to assert himself, despised criticism when it was unjust, spent all his fortune for Greece, and pursued with great perseverance his schemes for the civilization of his country. No man ever possessed more valuable qualities; he was extremely well informed, an indefatigable worker, loyal, simple in manner, and free from affectation and ceremoniousness. To all these admirable qualities he united a perfect trust in Providence." The Senate, after having succeeded in calming the fury of the people, which seemed likely to proceed to violent excesses, nominated a commission of government consisting of three members—Colettes, Colocotrones, and Avgoustos Capo d'Istria; the latter was elected President temporarily by the National Assembly convoked at Argos, until a congress should have been held. The new President was not recognized in the northern districts, and Colettes called together another National Assembly at Perakhora. The Roumeliotes marched upon Argos, and forced the President to resign (April 13th, 1832). Thiersch, the German philologist, then instituted a fresh governmental commission, until the arrival of Otho of Bavaria, the second son of King Louis I., who had been appointed to the throne by the three protecting Powers. The following was the basis of agreement : In return for an indemnity of twelve million francs, Turkey undertook to push back the boundaries as far as the Gulfs of Arta and Volo; Otho was allowed to contract a loan of sixty million francs under the guarantee of the three Powers; the

King of Bavaria undertook to furnish a body of troops, to the number of 3,500 men, to take the place of the troops of the Alliance hitherto stationed in Greece. Henceforth, Greece has existed as an Independent Kingdom.

CHAPTER VI.

CRETAN SONGS AND LEGENDS.

THE popular songs of Greece, in which the Greek nationality through many centuries of oppression has still preserved itself, may be divided into several classes.

I. *Historical.* Some of these go back as far as the tenth century, and deal with the heroic deeds of the *Akritæ*, or frontier-soldiers of the Byzantine Empire : the scene is usually laid in Asia Minor, or Mount Taurus. It is not, however, until the second half of the eighteenth century that they become numerous. The Cretan Revolution of 1770, brought about by the ambition of the Empress Catherine of Russia, was the origin of a number of songs, which are practically the only historical documents extant concerning the heroic struggles of that period on the island. Amongst them are *The Entry of the Turks into Sphakia,* and *Daskaloyiannes* (Master John) *of Sphakia.*

II. *Religious.* These comprise songs relating to the Church festivals, the Virgin Mary, the angels and saints, and, amongst the latter, St. George in particular, one of the most venerated saints in the Greek Church ; songs relating to various events connected with the life of Christ.

III. *Romantic.* These deal with the exploits of the *Klephts* (brigands), and romantic adventures generally.

IV. *Myrologia,* or funeral songs, of which there is a very large nnmber.

V. *Love Songs and Erotic distichs,* the latter almost exclusively confined to celebrating the charms of the lady. She is sometimes a rose, a pink, a pomegranate, an apple-tree loaded with fruit. When she passes along the street, it is filled with roses ; she is as white as the snow on the mountains, her head is a vessel of silver, her hair threads of silk, her eyes blue as sapphires or black as the Athenian olive, her mouth a half-open lily, her voice is as tuneful as that of the nightingale ; when she speaks, she restores the sick to health and brings back the dead to life ; she is a slender cypress, a flowering orange-tree, a hawk swift of flight, an eagle with golden wings, a ship proudly cleaving the waters. It is, however, only fair to add that the rejected lover does not, on occasion, shrink from calling his ladylove a "rotten sardine," "an old she-ass," or "a stinking kettle."

Most of the specimens of popular songs here submitted have their origin in Crete, and have all been translated* from the original Greek, where accessible.

I.

MASTER † JOHN OF SPHAKIA.
A TRUE STORY OF THE YEAR 1770.

Listen to me, both old and young, that I may tell and you may learn the story of Master John. Master John

---

* The translations are not to be considered as slavishly literal; abridgments have been made in some cases.

† The word here translated "Master" does not mean necessarily a "teacher" or "schoolmaster," but, like the Turkish Khoja, a "learned man," that is, a person who knew how to write.

of Sphakia, with your mighty army, did you not tell me that you would restore the Greeks? Every Easter and Christmas you put on your hat and said to the chief priest, "I will bring the Russians." *

"Master John of Sphakia," said the priest, "remain quiet, as becomes us, lest the Sultan hear you and send the Turks against us." The Vizier † wrote a letter and sent it to the Sultan. "Long live my Lord! tell me what I am to do. Shall I burn Sphakia, or abandon it?" "Neither burn it nor abandon it; no one is to blame but Master John." "Now, Master John, you must be wary, that you may finish your work, and not abandon it."

Then the Turks considered the matter, and went forth to fight, to spoil all that the enemy possessed. They first gave battle at Seli, in the plain of Crapi, and the general cried to his standard-bearer, "Pisinakes, take the standard!" "No, by God, I will not go forward; I am afraid, for they are many. See the Christian dogs, all with swords in their hands."

One Friday morning, before mid-day, the Turks, sword in hand, took Sphakia. At Franco-Castello they set up their tents, and at Aradæna played martial strains. They set fire to Aradæna, and burned the monasteries: they had no respect or pity for such buildings. At Madara they took Master John, with all his family and his standard. Twelve servants of the Pasha took him, and bound him and carried him off; all along the road he did not cease to entreat them, promised them gifts, promised them money, which had been coined in his house during Holy Week: he promised them gifts,

---

* Then regarded by the Greeks as their natural liberators.
† The governor of the island was then called by this title.

promised them sequins, which lay in his house as thick as dust. He wept for his daughters, above all, for Mary. "O Mary, my beloved child, I brought you up on honey, but now your food shall be fermented rose-laurel. O Anthusa,* I clothed your feet with gilded shoes, but now you shall walk barefooted on the stones." "You are going, Master John ; when shall I expect you back ? Tell me, that I may keep the door open and the table laid." "I am going, Mistress John, but I cannot advise you ; they are taking me to Castro,† and perhaps I shall never return." When they led him past his deserted house, his eyes ran with tears like troubled streams. "My children," said he, "it would need five hundred purses to rebuild it as it was before." Then Pisinakes Achmet Aga turned round and said to them : "He is going to lose his head, and yet weeps for his house." When they led him past the Khan ‡ Bambali he asked for cold water, that he might drink it and die. And when they led him past the first tent, he asked the Kahveji § to give him some coffee with sugar ; and they brought him coffee in a porcelain cup, and a chibouk ‖ of jasmin, almost as tall as himself. And when they led him up the stairs of the Pasha's house, he looked right and left, and cried aloud : "Children, where are my friends, and where are my kinsmen ? They are going to take away my life on the Pasha's gibbet."

* "Flower," a common female name in Crete.
† Megalo-Castro, the modern Canea.
‡ A kind of inn.
§ Coffee-house keeper.
‖ Long pipe.

II.

THE ENTRANCE OF THE TURKS INTO SPHAKIA.

(1770.)

They said that the Turks would not enter Sphakia ·
but I see that they have entered it in wrath. On Friday,
the 1st of May, the Turks entered Sphakia, sword in
hand : the Turks entered Sphakia, cursed be the hour!
and ravaged our country, as they ravaged every other.
" O valiant towns of Callicratē and Askyfo, where
are your young men, that they may run like lions?
Where are your young men, your famous warriors, that
they may run like lions and seize the passes?" "They
are playing instruments of music down at Franco-
Castello ; at Anopolis * they are throwing up entrenchments : they are awaiting the Turks, and leap
for joy, because they are going to fight and display
their valour." When the Turks reached the market-
place, they sent a messenger to the Sphakiotes : " Come
and make your submission, become rayahs, for we will
take you prisoners, even though you are heroes ; come
and make your submission at the Sultan's feet, that he
may bestow upon you a handsome present, that he may
bestow upon you great privileges, and that you may be
distinguished beyond all other districts. We will exempt
you and your descendants from the laws for all time."

" We know your gifts, that bring naught but woe :
you have bestowed them in abundance upon the rest
of Crete. Wherefore, we would all rather perish than

* The "upper city."

offer submission and bring dishonour upon ourselves. O cruel renegades,* you have devoured the Christians: wherefore, we will live in freedom, and will never become rayahs."

When the Pasha heard these words he was greatly enraged, and told the Sphakiotes that he would reduce them to slavery. "Do your will, O Pasha, and wait no longer; we will not submit, for we have sworn it. We will not submit to become rayahs; we all prefer death."

"Well, then, O Sphakiotes, I will send my army against you, and we will not depart as long as the summer lasts. You think that you will be safe upon the mountains; I also have foot soldiers: prepare to receive them. You have concealed your children in holes, but I will seize them, and carry them off to be my slaves."

"Take the women and children, take also the maidens; you may perhaps succeed, for you are renegades."

Such were their last words; after which they began a terrific combat from behind their entrenchments. When they opened fire and lighted the matches of their guns the bullets fell everywhere like claps of thunder, and smote their breasts like hail, and the blood ran in streams, like water from a spring.

Alas! how many braves fell, smitten to earth, so altered that none could recognize them! They lay on the ground, beautiful as angels, bathed in blood; they

---

The original word *Bourmas* signifies one who wears a turban. After the Turks conquered Crete, the inhabitants took to wearing the turban— the children who sprang from the union of the Turkish conquerors with the native Cretan women were, of course, not genuine Turks—and for this reason the Turks of Constantinople looked with contempt upon the Cretan Turks, and frequently called them " Bourmades," or "renegades."

lay there, and their mothers wept and lamented for them. With their gloomy tears they moved all hearts ; uttering mournful lamentations for the dead, with lips deadly pale they sat by their side, and sang their praises ; their groans ascended to Heaven, and on that day the flowers drooped and withered. This is all that they did, those famous men, to fall like wild beasts upon the infidels. And when the latter saw the fury of their enemies they hastened to flee, in peril of their lives.

All the Turks fled to Rethymnos,* to escape from the terrible slaughter, and the young rayahs asked them, "Where are your arms?" "The Sphakiotes have taken them, and have them in their possession." Then they asked them, "Where are your heroes?" "The Sphakiotes have devoured them on the mountains." Then they asked them, "Where are your commanders?" "The Sphakiotes have slain them all ; alas ! poor Agas ! "†

III.

ANTONIOS MELIDÓNES (1822).‡

Children, why are the birds so frightened? Has the hunter chased and slain them? No one has slain them, no one has chased them, no one has slain them. But they have heard that Captain Antonios has been slain. When he spoke, how valiant he was ! and suddenly they slew him unjustly, deeply to be mourned. When the news was brought to his master he rent his clothes, and flung them on the ground. " O All-powerful God, what

---

* Retimo, on the north coast.
† A Turkish word, a general term for " officer.
‡ See chap. iv.

manner of custom is this, to slay a man who has been guilty of no offence? O Captain Antonios, you who were like a flower, why did you not slay him with the pistol? O Captain Antonios, you who had no equal, why did you not slay him with the dagger? O Captain Antonios, beauteous youth, cursed be the Sphakiotes."

IV.

THE SONG OF ST. GEORGE.

(303.)

O holy George, my master, on your beauteous steed, with your sword girded round you, and wielding your golden spear, I fain would tell of your goodness and renown, you who slew the monstrous dragon, the beast which was at the spring, and devoured a man every morning and evening for its meal. Every day the lot decided upon whom it should fall to bring his child as a present to the monster. And it came about that, one day, the lot fell upon the King's only daughter, a maiden of surpassing beauty. When her father heard the terrible sentence, he was deeply grieved. "Take all I have," said he, "but leave me my child, my heart's delight." Then sharp swords were drawn, and his nobles said, "If you do not send your child, at any rate we will send you." "Take my child and deck her like a bride, take her as a present to the monster that he may feed upon her." Then they went and decked her out, from morning until evening, all in gold and pearls; she was like the sun in countenance, like the sea in her adornment, her pearls were as numerous as the sand.

And when they led her down the great staircase, her mother came forth, and exclaimed with a loud cry, and her father also came forth wearing his golden crown. The people accompanied her to the fountain, and the unhappy maiden never hoped to return. She shuddered, and her slender form trembled when she thought that the monster would devour her, poor girl, before her time. It happened that Saint George was passing along the street. "What seek you here, O maiden? why are you sitting in the forest?" "Go, young man, leave me, lest the monster devour you like myself." "Fear not the monster; I will slay him; let me rest my head upon your knees. When you hear the bellowing of the monster, fear not to wake me." When the maiden heard the noise of the monster coming to strangle her, in her fear she shouted out, "Help, Saint George!" And when he heard her, he ran to save her, and deliver her from the savage monster. Then he said, "Maiden, where did you learn my name? How do you know the saint?" "While you lay asleep, a dove flew to me with a golden cross in its right hand, and on the top of the golden cross was written, 'Saint George, whosoever wins his favour, never dies.'" The Saint sprang up and made the sign of the cross, hurled his spear at the monster and cleft his throat; then the monster fell to the ground, and the earth shook beneath him. Then he took off the chain of gold with which her neck was bound · "Henceforth, from to-day, have no fear of those fierce monsters." Afterwards he set her upon his horse, and went to the King's palace, and held converse with him. "Here is your daughter, O King; welcome your child, and from the chambers of your heart give her your blessing." "Long life to you, my knight; but tell me your name, that I may bestow upon you a royal gift." "Those of Scarpathia call me Soldier George; if you would make me a present, build a church; and on the left and on the right of it represent the likeness of a horseman, that all Christians may worship."

V.

War Song.

By Constantinos Rhigas.

How long, my braves, shall we live in the passes alone, like lions on the cliffs and on the mountains? how long shall we dwell in caves, and look upon naught but the forests? Shall we flee from the world to escape cruel slavery? leave parents, brothers, and country, friends, children, and kinsmen?

Better is one hour of a life of freedom than forty years of slavery and captivity. What good is life, if it is lived in slavery? Remember how they torture you every hour. Even though you be vizier, interpreter, or prince, the tyrant will unjustly compass your death. You toil as he orders you throughout the day, while he looks for the chance to drink your blood. Soutsos, Mourouzes, Petrakes, Skanaves, Ghikas, Mavrogenes are the mirror in which you may look and see. Brave captains, priests, laymen, and Agas are slain by the sword of injustice, and countless others, both Turks and Greeks, have lost their lives and property without any reason.

Come, let us all, fired by the same zeal, take an oath this day upon the cross; let us select men distinguished for love of their country; let the law be our first and only guide; let one man be the ruler of the fatherland, for anarchy differs not from slavery, but one man devours another, like so many wild beasts; then, with hands uplifted to Heaven, let us pour forth our hearts to God.

O King of the Universe, I swear by thee that I will never submit to the will of the tyrants; that I will never serve them, nor be deceived by them; that I will never trust their promises, as long as I live in the world; my fixed and only aim will be to destroy them; faithful to my country, I will break its bonds, and I will never desert my general. If I violate my oath, may the heavens thunder and lighten, consume and scatter me like a vapour.

In the east, in the west, in the north, in the south, let us all have one heart for our country. Bulgarians, Albanians, Servians, and Greeks, islanders and dwellers on the mainland, let us all with one impulse gird on the sword for the sake of liberty; let the news go forth, how valiant we are; let all who understand the art of war hasten hither, that they may overcome the tyrants. Here Greece calls upon them with open arms, offering them support, a resting-place, rank and honour. How long will you remain in the service of foreign kings? Come, and be the support of your own nation. It is better to die for your country than to hang golden tassels on your swords for a foreigner.

Souliotes and Mainiotes, famous lions, how long will you sleep, shut up in your caverns? Leopards of the

Black Mountain, eagles of Olympus, hawks of Agrapha, become one soul. Christian brethren, dwellers on the banks of the Danube and the Save, present yourselves, each and all of you, with arms in your hands ; let your blood boil with just indignation ; both small and great, vow the destruction of tyranny. Men of Macedonia, hurl yourselves like wild beasts upon the foe, and shed the blood of the tyrants at once. Dolphins of the sea, dragons of the islands, pour forth like lightning, smite the foe. Sea-birds of Hydra and Psara, it is time to listen to the voice of your country. You, its worthy scions who serve in the fleet, the law bids you launch forth fire. With one heart, with one mind, with one soul, smite, let the tyrant be uprooted. Let us light a flame throughout Turkey, that may travel from Bosnia to Arabia. Raise the cross above your banners, and smite the enemy like a thunderbolt. Do not imagine that he is strong ; his heart beats and he trembles like a hare. Three hundred Klephts showed him that, in spite of all his cannons, he could not withstand them.

Why, then, do you tarry ? Why stand as if you were dead ? Awake, be no longer divided, as if you were enemies. Just as our ancestors roused themselves like lions, and rushed into the thick of the fight for freedom's sake, so let us, O brothers, all take up arms at once, and rid ourselves of this cruel slavery. Let us slay the wolves who impose the yoke, and dare to tyrannize cruelly over the Greeks. Let the cross shine over land and sea ; let justice come, and the enemy disappear ; let the world be delivered from the frightful scourge that we may live free, O my brothers, upon the earth.

VI.

THE TWO BROTHERS.*

A merchant was coming down from the heights of the mountains, leading twelve he-mules and fifteen she-mules. Some brigands met him in the midst of the road, and seized the mules, that they might unload them and see whether there was any money concealed in the bags. But the merchant begged them not to unload the animals. "Ah! do not unload my poor mules! for my chest is sore from loading and unloading them!" Then the chief of the brigands was enraged, stopped, and said to him: "Look at this son of a dog, who does not weep for his own wretched life, but weeps for his mules. Where are you, my braves?" he cried; "give him a thrust with the sword, that he may remain where he is." But the brigands had compassion upon him because he was brave. So the captain flung himself upon the man like a savage lion; he drew his sword and stabbed him in the side. Then the merchant groaned deeply, and cried aloud with all his might, "Where are you, O my father? look upon me. Where are you, O my mother? weep for me." "Whence comes your mother? I will write her a letter." "My mother is from Arta, my father is from Crete; and I had an elder brother, who became a brigand." Then the captain shuddered, and took him in his arms; in his arms he bore him, and carried him to the physician's: "You have healed many that have been stabbed and wounded; heal this young

* This little poem explains itself; it is inserted as being probably of Cretan origin.

K

man also, for he is my brother." "We have healed many that have been stabbed and wounded, but wounds like these none could heal." Then the merchant begged his brother to take the mules : " Here, take the mules to our father !" " Ah, how can I say to our father and our own poor mother, ' I have killed my brother and taken his mules ' ? "

VII.

GEORGIOS SCATOVERGA.*

(1806.)

He who is a good listener is also a good story-teller, if he has a good memory. I also have listened, and have composed a Georgiad, the subject of which is " Georgios Scatoverga of the Plain." As I do not know how to read, in order that I may not forget this story, I have put it into the form of a song, that I might be able to remember it well.

Georgios was born at Mokhos ; his parents were peasants ; poor, a mere husbandman, he never learned to read. When he grew up, he repaired to Castro,† swift and wide awake as the morning star. He grew up in a foreign land, and became a brave, highly favoured in strength and boldness. When a Turk provoked him, he drew his sword, and returned it to his scabbard with bloodstained hand. He slew many Turks, and gained great renown, and he will enjoy immortal glory in Paradise. Several times he escaped and fled from the

---

* One of the most famous Cretan Klephts. The piece in the original is an excellent specimen of the Cretan dialect.

† Megalo-Kastro, Candia.

toils, but on one occasion he was thrown into prison, where he heard the mournful news that Arif Moshoghlu, in the plain of Crete, had assembled the young girls to dance before him, and had ordered his parents, amongst the rest, to send him their daughter. When the dance was over, Arif would have carried her off, but she escaped. Arif went to her father's house in the morning, and found her father weaving a net ; he sent him off to perform forced labour,* and in the mean time threatened his daughter, who felled him to the ground and deprived him of his arms. Then the Turk promised he would do her no harm, and asked her to give him back his arms ; she had no sooner done so than the infidel, like a furious serpent, slew her. When her father returned and crossed the threshold, he saw his daughter lying dead, and cried out, " What is that ? " Then the Turk killed him also, and looked about for others whom he might slay, but, finding none, returned to Castro. This is what Georgios heard in his prison in The City,† from which he at last, with great difficulty, escaped. Collecting assistance from his fellow-countrymen, he purchased arms of good quality, and, setting out from there, approached the coasts of our island of Crete, and entered a little harbour, which they call Malia. He hastened at once to his house, opened his father's tomb, and from his body took a ball, with which he loaded his gun ; then he sat down at table, playing on the lyre day and night, and practising with his pistols. When Moshoghlu heard of it, he set forth, intending to kill him, and sent orders to him to visit

---

* Angaria, the *corvée*.
† Constantinople, Stamboul.

him.   Georgios replied that he knew his house too well, and that Moshoghlu could come to him if he had anything to say to him.   Then Arif, taking twelve other Turks with him to assist him, went in search of Georgios, who was playing with his brother.   They told him that they also had come to drink.   They sat down at table, and the mother of Georgios poured out wine for them to drink ; when it was all consumed, they sent to the inn to fetch more.   In the mean time Arif asked him if he knew him, and told him if he loved him he should go and find him, and drink.   Georgios answered and said to him, " How could I love him when I see neither my father nor my sister at home ? "   " Poor fool, it is I who killed them, and I will kill you also."   " And I am come to give you the reward which you deserve."   Then Georgios fired at him with the bullet which he had drawn from his father's body, and gave it back to him to whom it belonged ; then he shot him again, this time through the heart.   In the disturbance the lamp went out. Georgios leaped from the place where he was, dealing blows right and left with his sword.   He wounded seven or eight of his assailants, but, his brother being wounded in the foot, he drew him by the hand, and thrust him outside, took him upon his shoulders, and set off for the woods and mountains.   Arif and four others fell dead, on the spot where the father and sister had been murdered.   Georgios went to Ephesus, and, when his brother recovered, he determined to return home.   Hadji Mustapha, a valiant Turk, famous and renowned for his deeds of slaughter, heard of it.   One day he waited for Georgios upon the road, with an Arab slave, and the servant of another Turk.   He saluted him courteously, and invited him to his house that he might enjoy himself. Mustapha was walking in front, Georgios followed him, the Arab was next, the Turkish slave last. The Arab had orders to fire upon Georgios from behind. But Georgios perceived the raising of the pistol ; he already had his own in his hand, and, almost before you had time to turn round to look, he had laid him low, and, with a second shot, had shot the Aga through the heart. The Turkish servant fled ; Georgios had been wounded in the arm by the Arab. He returned to Ephesus to recover from his wound, where he was put to death by poison. Thus, I have composed this little history, and I sing it to the accompaniment of my lyre for my amusement, and in hope of comforting a sorrowing heart. This story was composed entirely by Manuel, son of Hieronymus the priest.

VIII.

GLEMEDHES ALI.*

(1822.)

No man has ever yet been found to discover the truth, whether the commander at Loutro judged aright. He sent a firman to the district of Rethymnos, that Glēmēdhēs Ali, the man of war, should be seized. He drew his sword, and approached his assailants, who all attacked him like swallows. A Sphakiote rushed upon the foe, swift as a dove, and cut off his head with his right hand ; he cut off the head of Glēmēdhēs Ali and held it up in his hand like a flag. The head of the famous Glēmēdhēs, stained with blood, was carried to

* A native Cretan Mohammedan leader. The *dh* is pronounced like *th* in *this*, *that*.

Roussos,* who took two sequins, and bestowed it upon them as a reward, because they had slain Glēmēdhēs himself. For he had brought sorrow to many hearts and would have brought yet more ; may he who laments his death lose the sight of his eyes ! O Glēmēdhēs, alas for that head which once dared to go out to battle at Rethymnos and Canea ; O Glēmēdhēs, that head which once you adorned with flowers, is now in the hands of the Sphakiotes, a mark for their rifles. O Turks and Janissaries, gather together in the mosque, that you may look upon Glēmēdhēs Ali, the handsome brave.

IX.

THEODOROS.†

(1822, 1823.)

The commander sent him a written order, that no Turk should remain where the Greeks lived ; his mother also had bidden him fight bravely, and not suffer an Arnaout steed to escape. He went down to Servili and set up his tents, and went down to Gazi, where they amused themselves with sports. He slew many Turks, the holy terror of all ; but the Turks were many, and he was weary. " The men of Mylopotamos, though thick as the glades in the forest, if you resist them throughout the day, will flee when the sun goes down. O unhappy Anœanians and Chrysaniotes, who fight against the Turks as bravely as the Lakiotes. Woe is me, my poor brother ! why did I send you away ? You could have

---

* A Christian captain, from Askyfo.

† A Christian leader, who was slain during the revolt in a charge of the Arnaout cavalry.

assisted me to gain a refuge. Woe is me, my poor brother! would that you could hear how I have been slain to-day ; but you have no news of it. Greet the Sphakiotes from me and all the braves, and tell them how the Arnaouts have overthrown me."

X.

TZELEPES.

(Same date as preceding.)

Sorrow betide that Sunday and accursed be the Tuesday, when Tzelepes came here to fight. He sought Gaoures at the height of the cross, and he dragged his cannon to fight against the Turks. He drew his sword to pierce the roof, that he might hurl fire upon them and consume them all. Then Zounalakes fired, and so true was his aim that the ball entered Tzelepes's breast ; it entered his breast and reached his throat, and then Tzelepes cried, "Mercy." "Get up, Tzelepes, that we may make an attack ; maybe the Turks will come forth from the house." They went and buried him in the chief town of the Sphakiotes, because his renown smelt sweet as a violet. When evening came, the Turks came forth, not knowing that Tzelepes lay on his bier.

XI.

HADJI MIKHALES.

(1828).

On every Easter and Sunday, on every great festival, listen, that I may tell you of Hadji Mikhales. The men of Grabusa sat down and wrote an urgent message, they sent it to the Morea, inviting Hadji Mikhales. They also wrote to the Hadji, the ancient of the Morea, that he should get together horses and go down to Crete. At Anapli he collected sixty-five horsemen to go down to Crete, where the Egyptians were. After he had gathered his men together, he put them on board ships of war ; he had chosen Roumeliotes, handsome braves. He went, and, after landing all his men on the deserted coast of Grabusa, asked the inhabitants whether they had powder. "We have powder and bullets to fight with ; we only need your horses to go out into the plain." But he did not feel confident, and went to his boats, intending to disembark at Loutro, and learn the truth. There he found the Sphakiotes, valiant men, who were held in honour for their warlike deeds. "Come, O Sphakiotes, let the Rhizites come, that we may go and stir up the Catomerites. Come, O Sphakiotes, you who are braves, that we may fight against Turkey, and leave your flocks." When the Pasha heard this, he was sorely grieved—to Castro and Rethymnos came the news. "Gather together, O foremost braves of Turkey, that we may go and drive him back into the mountain districts. For either he will perish on the mountain districts, or he will fall into the sea, or we will kill him because he has come to us as it were a gift." When his Kiaya * heard this, he turned round and said, "O Mustapha Pasha, this man will not flee, for he is a brave. He is no Lazopoulos, to make for the mountain districts, but he is from Roumelia, and brings braves with him. He also brings youths from Bulgaria, honoured horsemen, and they will slay us, however cautious we may be." "Hush !

* The Vizier's deputy.

Pasha ; praise not to me sixty horsemen ; I will devour them like a salad or anchovies." So spake the Pasha, and that same hour he gathered together all his forces that he might go forth from the city. He ordered the Castrians to assemble, and the Rethymniotes to come and join the Caniotes ; to come and join them and form a column, and march to ravage the city of the Sphakiotes. They marched and collected their forces at the Hellenic arch ; the sons of Greece heard it and made for the mountain districts. Then Kyriakoules, a man of well-proved valour, who was held in high honour for his warlike deeds, said : " Grasp your swords, your weapons, and daggers at once, that we may rush upon the Turks. Maybe the Turks will fear when we make the attack ; maybe we shall drive them outside the entrenchments." And when he came to the mountain heights of Askyfo, all were decking the Turkish standards with flowers. And when the Sphakiotes saw them, they all exclaimed, both small and great, " O Hadji, go not to battle, for you are our head. You are our head, you are our honour, and if they kill you, our lives are lost." " As once I was born, so once will I die, and once I will bid farewell to the world above. It is better that they should kill me ; it is better that I should die, than that I should live disgraced in the world above. If the Pasha kills me, he will cut off my head and take it to Canea, and my honour with him ; or, if I kill him, I will cut off his head, and take it to the Morea, and take his honour with me. Saddle my horse, that I may go forth to battle. I hear the Pasha is coming, let me go and take him." Then he offered up a prayer, made the sign of the cross, took his light sword, and hung it round his neck. Then again he offered up a prayer, took his pistol, and placed it in his belt. When he had mounted into the saddle, even his horse wept, and then he knew that he should die. "To-day I shall be slain, this very day, that they may remember me in all the fortresses." He again offered up a prayer, leaped into his saddle, lashed his horse, and rode out of the gate.

XII.

THE CONDEMNATION OF CRETE.

In the year one thousand eight hundred and twenty-eight—listen, that I may tell you about the distressful island of Crete. The princes assembled and went to Paris, that they might hold a meeting to settle what was to become of Crete. After they had assembled and began the discussion, they were divided into parties, and gave it to the Turk. Then they sent a deputy, who went to bear the news to the Christians. When they were gathered together, he read the agreement, and told them how they had handed Crete over to the Egyptian. The Christians lamented and cried aloud: "O Lord commander, go up into the hills and sit in the roads; there you will see birds flying with the bones of Christians in their mouths. Who could tell you, who could number all who have perished on the mountains and in the groves? Listen, O Lord, let me tell you our sufferings. The Turks have sold our children into slavery in Arabia: all of us who were left ran to the hills, naked and barefooted, in order that we might obtain our freedom. We had confidence in you, the

Kings of the Franks, and now you will do us injustice and leave us slaves. When the terrible Judge shall come to judge us all, surrounded by all the hosts of heaven ; when He hears of the unjust sufferings of the Christians, when the Cretans come with their complaints and stand before the terrible Judge, then, O France and England, you shall answer before the terrible Judge, at the second coming." "What can I do for you, poor fools ? Why do you not write to the princes ? They have held a consultation, and agreed that Crete shall be handed over to the Egyptian. I am sorry for you, O Christians, I cannot help you : I cannot alter what has been determined."

Then came vessels of the Franks to Grabusa, and expelled the Christians who held it. They had on board Egyptians who overran the island, wearing red dresses and carrying drums. They settled in various places, and condemned and tyrannized over the Christians, and tortured the rayahs.

XIII.

THE LAY OF CHRISTOS MILIONES.[*]

(Probably end of seventeenth century.)

Three birds, settled on the heights above the haunts of the Klephts ; the first looked towards Armyros, the second in the direction of Valtos, while the third, the best of all, lamented and said · "My Lord, what has become of Christos Miliones ? He cannot be found at Valtos or Kryavrysis."[†] "We have heard that he has

---

[*] This song and the five which follow are taken from *Klephtic* ballads.
[†] Cold spring.

passed over to Arta, and has taken the Kadi prisoner with two Agas." The Turkish commander heard of it, and was greatly displeased. He called for Mavromates and Moukhtar of Kleisoura: "If you desire office, if you desire captaincies, kill Christos, the Captain Miliones. The Sultan has ordered it, and has sent a firman." Friday dawned, would that it had never done so! and Souleiman was sent to find Christos. He found him at Armyros, where they embraced like friends: throughout the night they drank, till break of day: and when dawn appeared, they went over to the quarters of the Klephts: "Christos, the Sultan demands your presence; the Agas also demands it." "While Christos lives, he will not surrender to the Turks." Then they charged each other with their muskets, fired at the same time, and both fell on the spot.

XIV.

THE LAY OF GYPHTAKES.

The plains thirst for water, the hills for snow, the hawks for birds, the Turks for heads. What has become of Gyphtakes's mother, who has lost two children, and her brother as well? And now she has gone mad, and walks about in tears. She is never seen, either in the plains or on the tops of the mountains. We have been told that she has gone on to Vlakhokhoria, where the sound of the gun is heard, rolling terribly. The noise of the firing was not heard at a wedding feast or religious holiday; Gyphtos had been wounded in the knees and the hand. He tottered like a broken tree, he fell like a cypress ; like the brave that he was, he cried with a loud voice, "Where are you, oh my brother, dearly beloved ? Come back, come back, take my head, that the troops of Yussuf, the Arabian, may not take it, and carry it to Yanina to that dog, Ali Pasha."

XV.

MOUNT OLYMPOS AND MOUNT KISSAVOS.

The two mountains, Olympos and Kissavos, quarrelled as to which of them should pour forth the rain, which the snow. Kissavos poured forth the rain, and Olympos the snow. Then Kissavos turned round and said to Olympos, " Do not quarrel with me, O Olympos, haunt of the Klephts ; I am Kissavos, famed at Larissa. Coniaria * takes delight in me, and the Agas of Larissa."

Then Olympos turned round and said to Kissavos, " Listen, Kissavos, listen, unseemly one, home of the Turks : I am old Olympos, famed throughout the world ; I have forty-two summits, sixty-two springs ; every spring has its standard, every branch has its Klepht ; on my highest peak an eagle has perched itself, holding in its claws the head of a brave. The eagle said to the head, 'O head, what have you done to be so despite-fully treated ?' The head replied, 'O bird, feed on my youth, feed on my bravery, that so you may make your wing an ell in length and your claw a span. At Louro,

* *i.e.* the Turkish nation.

at Xeromero, I was one of the Armatoli ; * at Khasia, on Olympos, I was for twelve years a Klepht ; I slew sixty Agas and burned their villages.   As for those whom I left on the spot, Turks and Albanians, they are too numerous, O bird, for me to count.   But at last my turn has come to fall in battle.' "

XVI.

The Klepht's Farewell.

Go down to the beach, go down to the shore : make your hands oars, your breast a rudder, your slender body a ship.   If God and the Holy Virgin desire that you should make your way to our quarters, where we hold counsel, where we once roasted the two goats, Floras and Tombras, and if the company should ask you anything concerning me, do not say that I have perished, poor unfortunate : say only that I have taken a wife in a strange country, that I have taken a flat stone for my mother-in-law, the black earth for a wife, and the little stones for my brother-in-law.

XVII.

The Klepht's Burial.

The sun was setting when Demos gave his orders : " Go, my children, fetch water, that you may take your evening meal.   Sit by my side, O nephew Lambrakes ;

* A body of armed Greeks, employed by the Turks to defend the mountain passes.   Their chief officer was called Kapitanos, and the district guarded by them, Kapitanaton.   When they quarrelled with the Turks, they became Klephts, or brigands.

come, put on my armour, and be a captain : and you, my boys, take my ill-fated sword, cut green branches, strew them as a seat for me, and go, fetch a confessor to whom I may confess and tell him all the sins that I have committed : thirty years I was one of the Armatoli, and twenty years a Klepht ; and now death has come upon me and I shall die. Make my tomb, make it wide and lofty, that I may stand upright and fight, and load my gun, leaning on my side. Leave a window on the right, that the swallows may come and bring me news of the spring, and that the nightingales may herald the gentle month of May.

XVIII.

ODE TO FREEDOM.

I recognize you by the terrible edge of your sword, I recognize you by your look, which so rapidly measures the earth.

Sprung from the sacred bones of the Hellenes, and vigorous as of yore, hail, Freedom, hail !

There you did dwell, carved with shame and bitterness, waiting for a voice to say to you, " Come forth again."

That day was long in coming, and silence reigned around ; men's hearts were terrified and oppressed by slavery.

Unhappy Freedom ! Nothing remained for you but to tell of your mighty past, and to tell of it with weeping.

You waited and waited for a freedom-loving voice, and wrung your hands in despair.

You said to yourself: "Ah! when shall I lift up my head from misfortune?" and, from above, you were answered by lamentations and groanings and bonds.

Then you lifted up your face, all besmeared with tears; blood trickled down your garment, Hellenic blood in streams.

With blood-stained garments, I know that you secretly went out to seek in foreign countries other powerful aid.

Alone you undertook the journey, alone you returned: doors do not open readily when necessity knocks at them.

One wept in your bosom, but gave you no respite; another promised * you assistance, and mocked you terribly.

Others—alas, for your pitiful lot!—exulted over your misfortune: "Go and find your children, go!" said the hardhearted wretches.

Your foot started back, and speedily trod the stone or turf, which preserves the remembrance of your glory.

Your head lies low in the dust, in deep humility, like the poor man who knocks at the door of the wealthy, and whose life is a burden to him.

Yes; but now † every son of yours is struggling valiantly against the foe, seeking, with inexhaustible courage, victory or death.

Sprung from the sacred bones of the Hellenes, valiant as of yore, hail, Freedom, hail!

No sooner did Heaven behold your efforts, the which,

* Catherine II., Empress of Russia.
† Written in 1824, during the height of the Revolution.

on the soil where you first saw the light of day, caused flowers and fruit to grow for your enemies—

Than it grew calm : a voice was heard proceeding from beneath the earth, and the martial voice of **Rhigas** answered you.

All countries saluted you with generous acclamations, and out of their hearts their mouths spoke.

The Ionian Islands cried until their voice reached the stars, and lifted up their hands in token of joy.

Although each of them * was bound with artfully-riveted fetters, and false freedom was engraven on their forehead.

The country of Washington was stirred to its very soul, and remembered the fetters in which she had once been bound.

The Spanish lion roared from his tower, as if saying, " Hail to you ! " and shook his fearful mane.

The leopard of England trembled with fright, and suddenly carried his threatening roar towards the confines of Russia.

He showed, by the rapidity of his movements, the mighty strength of his limbs ; and darted a fiery look upon the waves of the Ægean.

The eye of the eagle, which nourishes its claws and wings on the vitals of Italy, discovered you from the heights of the clouds.

But woe to him who, having come within reach of your sword, ventures to offer you resistance ! †

* At that time they were under a British protectorate.

† The dithyrambic poem, from which the above stanzas are selected, is by Dionysius Salomos (1798-1857), a native of Zante. This explains his antipathy to England. His Hymn to Freedom has been translated into nearly every language of Europe, no less than four having appeared in Italy.

Space does not permit of specimens of Myriologia, Love Songs, or Proverbs being given, but the insertion of the following curious legend (abridged in parts) will, it is hoped, be excused. It is from the pen of Rhizos Rhangabes, one of the most prolific and accomplished writers of Modern Greece, and is well worth reproducing in English. The translator is not aware of its having been translated before. Similar stories are current in regard to the Devil's Bridge in Switzerland, bridges at Frankfort and Pont à Mousson, and Crowland Abbey in England.

THE DEVIL'S BRIDGE.

Once upon a time there was a Pasha of Damala, who wanted to have a bridge made over the river, that he might be able to cross it when he went hunting. Many clever architects came from various parts of the Morea, and asked large sums of money, because the task was very difficult. Now, there lived at Damala a workman, who lived on charity, and was an idle and useless fellow. He envied his fellow-workmen from the Morea, abused them as strangers, and did not want to let them make any money. So he went to the Pasha, and told him that he would build the bridge better for half the money, and, as he made a great disturbance, the Pasha gave him the commission, on condition, however, that if he failed he should lose his head. So the man built the bridge, and, when it was finished, declared boastfully that there was not its like in the world.

The same night the rain fell upon the mountains, the river swelled, and carried away the bridge. The man's terror was indescribable when he heard the Pasha give the executioner orders to cut off his head; he was in despair, because he knew that the next day would be his last. He was sitting in front of the fire in his cottage, when he suddenly heard steps by his side; on turning round, he saw a man standing by, clothed in black, with black eyes, beetle-browed, with a long nose and chin, and an inkstand in his girdle. The man humbly saluted him.

"Who are you, and where did you come from? My door was shut!"

"Excuse me. I heard you weeping, and came to ask you what was the matter, and to see if I could help you."

The architect told him what was the cause of his grief, and what he wanted.

"Is that all? That is very easy. The bridge shall be built as you want."

"Alas! it would be no good if you were to build it as strong as the citadel of Nanplia. I shall lose my head to-morrow, because the bridge has fallen in."

"We have the whole night before us," said the man dressed in black. "The bridge shall be built; what else can I do for you?"

"To tell you the truth, my other desire is to be rich, and that immediately."

"I am at your orders. Anything else?"

"I am much obliged for your kindness. And now tell me how I can serve you."

"You need not trouble yourself," said the other, politely. How many years longer would you like to live?"

"If I could live three years in the manner I desire, I should be content."

"Three years, then," answered the stranger, with a deep obeisance. "I have only one little souvenir to ask of you: after the three years, I will ask you to give me your soul."

"My soul! Oh, that is a serious matter. It seems to me that, even when I am dead, I shall want my soul."

"Oh, that alters the case. I don't want to force you. I am sorry I cannot help you or give you the wealth you desire. However, you have no need of it, for to-morrow the Pasha will cut off your head."

"Ah, you are right; I had forgotten that," said the builder, deathly pale. "I don't want to give my head to the Pasha; can't you help me?"

"I am quite ready to serve you; only—your soul at the end of three years. Come, I will give you six, to oblige you."

The builder agreed. Then the unknown pulled a little book out of his pocket, dipped his finger-nail, which was long and pointed, into the inkstand instead of a pen, drew up the agreement, set down the date, the 25th of December, and gave it to the builder to sign. The builder did not know how to write, and offered to make the sign of the cross. Then the stranger flew into a passion, and began to foam at the mouth and tremble in his rage, and the builder dipped his finger in the inkstand, and made his mark. The unknown put the book back into his pocket, saluted the builder humbly, bade him farewell, and vanished.

The next day the builder went to the mountain, and, when he looked up, his amazement was indescribable;

for, high above his head, where the eagles only could reach, and where the torrent, even if it overflowed, would never reach the bridge, where only the spirits of the air could have been the builders, he saw a bridge that spanned the two mountains. While descending the mountain, in his haste to go and tell the Pasha, he found a jar full of gold pieces. Having stored his newly-found wealth in a place of safety, he ran to the Pasha, who, when he saw the bridge, marvelled, and declared him the chief architect in the Morea and the whole world.

From that time the worthy man lived highly honoured in the midst of luxury, and was made President of the town. The years went on, and the world was full of stories of his wealth and extravagance.

One Christmas Day he went out from Damala without saying where he was going. He was going to take some gold pieces from his inexhaustible store. He went, and returned no more. The herdsmen who were feeding their flocks on the mountains, afterwards related that they had seen him crossing the bridge ; that a mighty storm of wind had arisen, that the sky grew as dark as pitch, the wind howled on the cliffs, and blew as if it would have torn the mountain up by its roots. Then rain and hail fell, and the lightning flashed, and in the midst of the thunder they heard loud shouts of laughter in the air, and when the sky cleared the architect was no longer on the bridge, and was no longer to be seen. When they passed on to the place where they had last seen him, all that they found was a piece of blackened paper, with characters written upon it, which not one of the most learned men in Damala could read.

THE END.

Jarrold & Sons, Printers,
Norwich, Yarmouth, and London.

New 6s. Novels.

Crown 8vo, Art Linen, Gilt Top.

1. ## The Power of the Dog.
   By ROWLAND GREY, Author of "In Sunny Switzerland," "By Virtue of His Office." 2nd Edition.

2. ## Black Diamonds.
   (Authorised Edition.) By MAURUS JÓKAI, Author of "'Midst the Wild Carpathians," "In Love with the Czarina," "Pretty Michal," etc. 3rd Edition.

3. ## Judy a Jilt.
   By MRS. CONNEY, Author of "A Lady Housebreaker," "Gold for Dross," etc. 2nd Edition.

4. ## Lady Jean's Son.
   By SARAH TYTLER, Author of "Lady Jean's Vagaries," etc. 2nd Edition.

5. ## Colour Sergeant No. 1 Company.
   By MRS. LEITH ADAMS, Author of "Bonnie Kate," "Louis Draycott," etc. 2nd Edition.

6. ## The Inn by the Shore.
   By FLORENCE WARDEN, Author of "A House on the Marsh," etc. 4th Edition.

7. ## The Green Book, or Freedom Under the Snow.
   By MAURUS JÓKAI, Author of "Black Diamonds," etc. 3rd Edition.

8. ## My Bonnie Lady.
   By LESLIE KEITH, Author of "'Lisbeth," etc. [*Shortly*

9. ## The Winds of March.
   By GEORGE KNIGHT, Author of "Dust in the Balance," "Sapphira of the Stage," "The Circle of the Earth," etc. [*Shortly*

The Captive of Pekin, or the Swallow's Wing.
By CHARLES HANNAN. Graphically Illustrated by A. J. B. SALMON. New Edition. [*Shortly*

LONDON : 10 & 11 WARWICK LANE, E.C.

Messrs. Jarrold and Sons'

"GREENBACK" SERIES OF POPULAR NOVELS

BY AUTHORS OF THE DAY.

In crown 8vo, cloth, 3s. 6d. each.

By HELEN MATHERS.

Cherry Ripe!
Story of a Sin
Eyre's Acquittal
My Lady Green Sleeves
Jock O'Hazelgreen
Found Out!
Murder or Man-
      slaughter?
The Lovely Malincourt

By CURTIS YORKE.

That Little Girl
Dudley
Hush!
Once!
A Romance of Modern
      London   [teau
The Brown Portman-
His Heart to Win
Darrell Chevasney
Between the Silences!
A Record of Discords
The Medlicotts
The Wild Ruthvens

By MRS. LEITH ADAMS.

Bonnie Kate
Louis Draycott
Geoffrey Stirling
The Peyton Romance
Madelon Lemoine
A Garrison Romance

By IZA DUFFUS HARDY.

A New Othello!

By SCOTT GRAHAM.

The Golden Milestone
A Bolt from the Blue

By T. W. SPEIGHT.

The Heart of a Mystery
In the Dead of Night

By MRS. H. MARTIN.

Lindsay's Girl

By E. M. DAVY.

A Prince of Como

LONDON: 10 AND 11, WARWICK LANE, E.C.

"GREENBACK" SERIES OF POPULAR NOVELS

—CONTINUED.

In crown 8vo, cloth, 3s. 6d. each.

By ESMÉ STUART.
Harum Scarum

By AGNES MARCHBANK.
Ruth Farmer

By J. S. FLETCHER.
Old Lattimer's Legacy

By MAJOR NORRIS PAUL.
Eveline Wellwood

By
SOMERVILLE GIBNEY.
The Maid of London
Bridge

By MRS. A. PHILLIPS.
Man Proposes

By MARGARET MOULE.
The Thirteenth Brydain

By MRS. E. NEWMAN.
The Last of the Haddons

By EASTWOOD KIDSON.
Allanson's Little Woman

By ELEANOR HOLMES.
Through Another Man's
Eyes

By LINDA GARDINER.
Mrs. Wylde

By MRS. BAGOT HARTE.
Wrongly Condemned

By FERGUS HUME.
The Lone Inn   [Court
The Mystery of Landy
The Mystery of a Han-
som Cab
The Expedition of
Captain Flick

By LE VOLEUR.
By Order of the Brother-
hood!

By JOHN SAUNDERS.
A Noble Wife

By E. BOYD BAYLY.
Jonathan Merle
Alfreda Holme   [ture
Zachary Brough's Ven-
Forestwyk

By EVELYN
EVERETT GREEN.
St. Wynfrith and its
Inmates

By MRS. HAYCRAFT.
Gildas Haven

By HUDE MYDDLETON.
Phœbe Deacon

LONDON: 10 & 11, WARWICK LANE, E.C.

New 6s. Novel.

Crown 8vo, Art Linen, Gilt Top.

The Green Book. By MAURUS JÓKAI, Author of "Black Diamonds," " 'Midst the Wild Carpathians," "Pretty Michal," etc. Translated into English by Mrs. Waugh (Ellis Wright), with portrait of Dr. JÓKAI. (Authorised Edition.) Fifth Edition.

Mr. W. L. Courtney, in the *Daily Telegraph* says:—"No preface or apology is needed for the new novel of Maurus Jókai, 'The Green Book. It is a truly astonishing book, the latest novel, dealing with the early years of the present century, and with that world of inarticulate romance, the Empire of all the Russias.

"All the superficial culture and essential barbarism of the country are depicted in these pages. We see how the Moujik alternately plots and trembles, how the Tsar himself is checked in all his noblest aspirations by the iron framework of a society to which he is really slave, and Imperial conventions which he is powerless to break through. Jókai, in force and fire and prodigal variety, reminds one of the elder Dumas."

The *Daily Chronicle* says:—"The Author has given us a group of striking personalities, every one of whom is brilliantly drawn and vividly presented. All Jókai's very remarkable powers of characterisation, of individualising, are displayed here as strongly as in anything he has ever written. The historic moment chosen is an extremely dramatic one. The scenes are laid in Russia, at the end of the first quarter of the present century, when Russian society and the Imperial army were seething with revolutionary emotion, and St. Petersburg was a nest of intrigues. Jókai has a rare faculty of seeing all round his characters, of penetrating rough exteriors, and of probing to whatever of genuine human fibres they may have. From every point of view, 'The Green Book' is a book to be read. It is an interesting and knowledgable narrative of a puzzling, political period; and it is a work of fine art."

The *Bookseller* says:—"In no other novel has the author attained the vivacity, the wit, the dramatic contrivance exemplified in this romance. The scene between the Imperial Censor (of morals) and the artist employed upon Arakhscieff's palace might have come straight out of Molière. The conjecture of Sophie's funeral and Bethsaba's wedding are worthy of the elder Dumas. Then what a touch of nature is that where Sophie discovers that her own pretended is her mother's lover."

The *Aberdeen Free Press* says:—"Another work by Jókai, made accessible to English readers, is a literary event of more than common note. 'The Green Book' will be found an excellent specimen of the novelist's work, marked as it is by the best characteristics of Jókai's soaring genius. It is a series of brilliant, dramatic episodes, strung together by slender threads of love and political intrigue. Nowhere will one find better examples than in 'The Green Book' of Jókai's deep and expansive imaginative power."

The *Eastern Daily Press* says:—"A Russian historical romance, cast in vigorous and original mould, and full of that realistic power and picturesque description, which give Dr. Jókai a place in the front rank of popular writers."

LONDON : 10 & 11 WARWICK LANE, E.C.

New 6s. Novel.

Crown 8vo, Art Linen, Gilt Top.

The Inn by the Shore. By FLORENCE WARDEN, Author of "Pretty Miss Smith," "A Prince of Darkness," "A House on the Marsh," "A Perfect Fool," etc. 4th Edition.

The *Academy* says :—" Miss Florence Warden is unrivalled in a certain department of fiction. 'The Inn by the Shore' exhibits her at her best. It is full of marvellous mystery; and to the credit of the author, it must be confessed that the clue to the mystery is exceedingly difficult to find in advance."

The *Daily News* says :—" A story of mystery and crime, from the pen of Miss Florence Warden. Who perpetrates the robberies in the solitary inn by the shore? Whose is the soft little hand that in the dead of night skilfully extracts from under the visitor's pillow the watch and purse he has hidden there? On a wintry evening at the fireside, one might do worse than spend an hour in seeking to puzzle it out. The story provides sensations that will satisfy those who care for an uncritical shudder."

The *New Age* says :—" We can heartily recommend as a certain remedy for ennui, and as a companion in moments when you may have a vacant or a pensive mood, without anything to rejoice either the outward or inward eye, Miss Florence Warden's new and interesting story. It is a capital tale in every respect. From the first page to the last, the story is brightly and crisply written."

Punch says :—" A clearly-told and alluringly-exciting story."

The *Literary World* says :—" 'The Inn by the Shore' is full of sensational reading, and, can expect to find a large measure of favour with those who favour stories of crime and its unfolding."

The *Dundee Advertiser* says :—" Readers acquainted with Florence Warden's 'House on the Marsh' will not require to be pressed to take up her new novel. It is fully as romantic and entertaining as its famous predecessor. The broad effect of the tale is extremely successful."

The *Belfast Evening Telegraph* says :—" The title of this work at once induces the reader to jump at conclusions, and those who take it up in the hope of tragedy and mysteries unravelled will not be disappointed. The unveiling of the mysteries is skilful: the whole story is well-conceived and successfully executed."

The *Sheffield Daily Telegraph* says :—" How Miss Warden skilfully weaves her plot, and as skilfully unweaves it, until we know the truth, makes up a tale with delightful and sustained interest, which the reader will enjoy."

LONDON : 10 & 11 WARWICK LANE, E.C.

The "Greenback" Series.

Crown 8vo, Cloth, 3s. 6d.

The Lovely Malincourt.

By HELEN MATHERS.   6th Thousand.

The *Scotsman* says :—"The novel deals with the cream or froth of fashionable life ; it has plenty of light and bright colouring, and yet does not lack an undertone of earnestness, and is healthy and amusing."

The *Morning Leader* says :—"' The Lovely Malincourt' is one of those dazzling phenomena that all men are startled by, and 'The Lovely Malincourt's' hero is one of those men that at least two women love at the same time."

The *Dundee Advertiser* says:—" To novel readers Helen Mathers is a name of happy memory, recalling as it does that fascinating story, 'Comin' Thro' the Rye.' The latest story from the same gifted pen is entitled 'The Lovely Malincourt,' and deals with fashionable life in London."

The *Liberal* says :—"The novels of Miss Helen Mathers are always delightful. Few authoresses of the present day excel her in the happy combination of a good plot, clearly drawn characters, a bright and oftentimes brilliant style, and a wit that is as genuine as it is untinged by vulgarity."

The *Hull News* says :—"The works of Miss Helen Mathers are like good wine and need no bush ; nor is her latest story, 'The Lovely Malincourt' any exception to her previous novels."

The *Western Daily Press* says:—" Any book by the talented author of 'Comin' Thro' the Rye,' is sure to attract many readers. There is always a certain freshness about her pages that makes them delightful. There is nothing but pleasant reading in the book, which is sure to find a host of admirers."

The *Whitehall Review* says :—" Everyone knows what to expect when they take up a novel by the author of 'Comin' Thro' the Rye.' Such cardinal virtues as refinement, delicacy and purity of tone, are hers particularly, and the most captious critic can find no weak spot in her literary armour. 'The Lovely Malincourt' is a distinctly readable book."

The *Lady's Pictorial* says :—" A new story from the bright and sympathetic pen of Helen Mathers is as refreshing and as welcome as rain in summer, and it was with real regret that I read the last page and put aside the volume."

The *Realm* says:—"' The Lovely Malincourt' is a charming story, told as only Miss Helen Mathers could tell it. One cannot read the book without falling in love with Leslie—and surely the book is a success when one falls in love with the heroine."

LONDON : 10 & 11 WARWICK LANE, E.C.

The "Daffodil" Library.

Vol. I.   *Narrow 8vo, Paper,* 1s. 6d. ; *Cloth,* 2s.

The Jaws of Death.

By GRANT ALLEN.   6th Thousand.

The *Daily Chronicle* says :—"'The Jaws of Death' is a pretty piece of writing in the sensational line. We are brought so smoothly, so gradually, to the very edge of the catastrophe, the shiver of it is upon us almost before we are there. It is extremely creditable to Mr. Allen's invention."

The *Daily News* says ·—"The whole thing is exceedingly well done."

The *Literary World* says :—"It does great credit to Mr. Grant Allen's vivid imagination and able descriptive powers."

The *Daily Courier* says :—"There are few authors who can write such good short stories as Mr. Grant Allen."

The *Scotsman* says :—"'The Jaws of Death' is an attractive story of a strange and exciting character, suitable for perusal on the sea-shore or the mountain side. A good-going story, with plenty of spirit, and not a little fun."

The *Bookseller* says :—"It is told in a fashion which makes the reader forget the improbability, and only feel regret that the end is reached all too soon."

The *St. James' Gazette* says :—"The climax is ingeniously arrived at, and the preliminary narrative is lively and entertaining."

The *Aberdeen Free Press* says :—"There are few better story-tellers than Mr. Grant Allen when he is in the vein, and in this little volume we have him at his best."

The *Western Mail* says :—"This dainty volume forms the first of the Daffodil Series. 'The Jaws of Death' is a clever little story from the pen of a distinguished novelist. It is intensely well told."

The *North British Daily Mail* says :—"We give the initial number of this series our most unqualified approval ; it is excellent from every point of view."

The *Belfast News Letter* says :—"No one with a taste for the humorous will deny that the author has tickled him with his picture of Howard Freke of Cooper's Pike ; and if he combine in his nature a love for the sensational, the closing chapters apropos of the doings of Li Sing cannot possibly fail to delight him equally. The story is most enjoyable throughout."

The *Bath Herald* says : — "The book is powerfully and dramatically written, and the volume is a welcome introduction to what is likely to become a very popular series."

LONDON : 10 & 11 WARWICK LANE, E.C.

The "Impressionist" Series.

Crown 8vo, Cloth, gilt, 3s. 6d.

Under this general heading Messrs. Jarrold and Sons propose to issue, from time to time, a volume of Short Stories. It is intended, so far as possible, to link story to story by some thread of mental connection, and, thus, to present to the reader a series of vivid and related pictures.

1. ## Dust in the Balance.
   By GEORGE KNIGHT. With Title Page and Cover Design by Laurence Housman.   2nd Edition.

2. ## Some Women's Ways.
   By MARY ANGELA DICKENS. With Title Page and Cover Design by Laurence Housman.   2nd Edition.

3. ## Blind Larry. Irish Idylls.
   By LEWIS MACNAMARA. With Title Page and Cover Design by Laurence Housman.

4. ## Sweet Audrey, or Comedies of Country Life and Town Glamour. By GEORGE MORLEY. [*Shortly*

The "Daffodil" Library.

A Series of Shorter Novels by Authors of the day, in convenient shape and attractive binding.

Narrow 8vo, paper covers, 1s. 6d.; cloth, 2s.

1. ## The Jaws of Death.
   By GRANT ALLEN.   6th Thousand.

2. ## Sapphira of the Stage.
   By GEORGE KNIGHT.   5th Thousand.

3. ## The Kaffir Circus, and other Stories.
   By M. DONOVAN.   4th Thousand.

4. ## Because of the Child.
   By CURTIS YORKE.   5th Thousand.

5. ## A Studio Mystery.
   By FRANK AUBREY.   [*Shortly*

LONDON: 10 & 11 WARWICK LANE, E.C.

Popular Holiday Books.

Poppyland.

Papers descriptive of Scenery on the East Coast. By CLEMENT SCOTT. Crown 8vo, cloth elegant, with 26 Illustrations by F. H. TOWNSHEND. Superior Edition, 2s. 6d. In attractive Paper Covers, 1s.

"It is not surprising that a fourth edition of Mr. Scott's delightful little book is called for. It deals with the charming coast of the far south-east of our island, and the epithet 'Poppyland' given to that has a poetic ring about it that is very attractive. The vicinities chiefly dealt with are Overstrand and its vicinity, Cromer, Lowestoft, and Yarmouth."—*The Queen*.

Summer in Broadland ; or, Gipsying in Norfolk Waters.

Fourth Edition. Profusely Illustrated by the Gipsies. Crown 8vo, Illustrated Paper Covers, 1s. ; or Superior Edition, cloth elegant, 2s. 6d.

The *Queen* says :—"A hardy manual based upon actual experiences. It is nicely illustrated, and is sure to please and instruct visitors to the Broads of East Anglia."

The *Scotsman* says :—"A delightful little volume, with many dainty illustrations, as a result of a holiday among the little-known Norfolk and Suffolk Broads. There are many capital descriptions of scenery, and the book is marked by bright and vigorous writing "

Sunrise-Land.

Rambles in Eastern England. By ANNIE BERLYN, Author of "Vera in Poppyland," etc. Illustrated by A. RACKHAM and M. M. BLAKE. 3s. 6d.

" Full of warm sympathy for picturesqueness and colour, written in an agreeable fashion, and evidently compiled from an intimate knowledge of the country and its inhabitants."—*Pall Mall Gazette*.

Two Knapsacks in the Channel Islands.

By JASPER BRANTHWAITE and FRANK MACLEAN, B.A., Oxon. Illustrated by VICTOR PROUT. Crown 4to, Pictorial cover, 1s.

JARROLD & SONS, 10 & 11, WARWICK LANE, LONDON, E.C.

Dr. Gordon=Stables' Health Manuals.

Crown 8vo, Cloth, 2/6 each. (Postage 4½d.)

Sickness or Health? or, The Danger of Trifling Ailments. 2nd Edition.

"The work is practical, and written in a readable style. It merits a place in every public and private library in the land. The publishers are to be warmly congratulated on the publication of this excellent volume."—*Hull Examiner.*

The Wife's Guide to Health and Happiness. 2nd Edition.

"This book reads like a novel, and is just as interesting as a novel, and far more instructive. The advice given is sensible, and up to date. Dr. Stables handles difficult and delicate subjects with great skill. A great deal of misery would be prevented if the young wife would adhere to the advice given in this book."—*The Medical Monthly.*

The Mother's Book of Health and Family Adviser. 2nd Edition.

"The Doctor, in his new book, has endeavoured to give in practical and clear language much valuable and essential information to mothers, and we believe that the manner in which he has treated this subject will be widely appreciated."—*The Sun.*

The Girl's Own Book of Health and Beauty. 2nd Edition.

"Teems with useful hints and good suggestions. Ought to be in the hands of every young woman."—*The Leicester Chronicle.*

The Boys' Book of Health and Strength.

2nd Edition. With portraits of DR. GORDON-STABLES, C.M., R.N., R. G. GORDON CUMMING (the Lion Hunter); W. McCOMBIE SMITH (Champion Scotch Athlete); J. D. MACPHERSON (Champion Putter); G. H. JOHNSTONE (Champion Hammer Thrower of Scotland); and *Special Letter to Boys* by W. McCOMBIE SMITH, the Champion Scottish Athlete.

"Such a common sense *vade mecum* to health and strength, should find a place on every boy's bookshelf."—*Star.*

JARROLD & SONS, 10 & 11, WARWICK LANE, LONDON, E.C.

Printed in Great Britain
by Amazon